THE 1962 INDIA - CHINA WAR: WHAT THEY DON'T WANT YOU TO KNOW

A Damning Expose On The Namka Chu Battle.

SANDEEP MUKHERJEE

© Sandeep mukherjee2022
All rights reserved

All rights reserved by author. No part of this publication may be reproduced, stored in a retrieval system or transmitted in any form or by any means, electronic, mechanical, photocopying, recording or otherwise, without the prior permission of the author.

Although every precaution has been taken to verify the accuracy of the information contained herein, the author and publisher assume no responsibility for any errors or omissions. No liability is assumed for damages that may result from the use of information contained within

First Published by

An Imprint of BlueRose Publishers
ISBN: 978-93-5704-022-8
Price:
Co-Author:
Editor:
Illustrator:
BLUEROSE PUBLISHERS
www.bluerosepublishers.com
info@bluerosepublishers.com
+91 8882 898 898

Dedication

"Only the dead have seen the end of war"- Plato

This work is dedicated to Captain Mahavir Prasad, Maha Vir Chakra (posthumous), who, in 1962, told the Indian Army where to go, what to do and what not to do in that place, and why. But soon the army sent him to that same wretched place to do those very things he had forbidden. He went there and fell in action, quietly doing what he had predicted would be 'suicidal' to try. And history just passed him by and consigned him to a footnote.

Here is to all the Mahavir Prasads of military history!

Acknowledgements

This book - project may not have seen the light of day but for certain individuals and institutions playing an enabling role.

Lt. General Harcharanjit Singh Panag, PVSM, AVSM (retired), former GOC in C of the Northern and Central Commands of the Indian Army, has acted as my mentor and guide, in de- fence and strategic affairs, for several years now.

The basic groundwork for this book emerged from a conver-sation I had one afternoon with Colonel Kanwaljeet Singh (Retired). His help made this research work possible.

Brigadier Indrajeet Gakhal (retired) appeared on my video series, Sandy Wars, on the YouTube Channel of India Sentinels, providing fundamental inputs on that fateful patrol of Captain Mahavir Prasad, MVC, (in May-June 1962) at the Namka Chu area.

I had a most enriching discussion with Lt General Ravi Eipe, PVSM, AVSM (retired), former GOC in C - Eastern Command of the Indian Army, who led a company of the 2 Rajput battalion, during the battle of Namka Chu.

Brigadier AJ.S. Behl (retired), who was the Gun Position Officer with E Troop, 17 Parachute Field Regiment, atop the Tsangdhar- Ridge, during the battle of Namka Chu, kindly shared with me, some of his invaluable personal recollections of the combat.

While talking of my debts to the Indian Veterans' Community, for this book, I have held back the name of Major General Krishen Khorana (retired) till the last. He played a key role with the 1 Sikh battalion on the Bumla - Tawang axis, resisting the Chinese advance on 23 October 1962. He made this account "real" by providing his personalized inputs on his friend and senior, Captain Mahavir Prasad, as a human being, the circumstances around the latter's patrol and the subsequent tragedy on the day of battle.

Finally, we come to the civilian "trooper" who made it all possible. Jayanta Bhattacharya, my friend, and Editor in Chief of the India Sentinels website on defense & strategic affairs. His encouragement, platforming of my work on Indian military history and his technical assistance in producing the videos for my 'Sandy Wars' series, provided the momentum for making this project real. He had carried the first shorter version of this work, on his website in 2021. He and my daughter Shankhabela, helped me in tidying up the manuscript of this book. My use of Google Earth's Satellite Imaging facilities enriched this work and would, hopefully, help my readers visualise what the area and terrain is like, in reality. The photograph on the cover page, of Indian troops surrendering to the Chinese in Nefa was taken by an unknown Chinese photographer. The source for the photo on the back page, showing Brigadier Dalvi being taken prisoner by the Chinese, has been mentioned below this image in chapter 5.

Foreword

1962 Conflict with China - a foreword.

This is a pain that doesn't leave us, the officers and men who fought in the Towang Sector in Nefa, that autumn and winter of 1962. Post the debacle, senior officers who handled the conflict, wrote personal accounts and exonerated themselves of any responsibility for the disastrous outcome. With time and awareness level of people leaping up, the quest for truth of the matter grew loud and louder - how the conflict came about and why did it end ignominiously for India. Some termed it as a national shame.

In that wave of truth seeking, almost inquisitional, few historians and analysts dedicated themselves to in-depth research of the Conflict - A to Z. This book, is a product of that dedication and I am tasked to write a foreword.

While I was privy to most events and happenings in the Kameng Frontier Division of Nefa (Arunachal), my battalion (1 SIKH), though originally a part of 7 Infantry Brigade, was later operationally deployed, in the right wing of 4 Division, on axis Bumla - Towang, under Brigadier Kalyan Singh's 4 Artillery Brigade, which came under Chinese assault on 23/24 October 1962. So, I didn't fight at Namka Chu, which was in the left wing.

Suffice it to say that on 20 October 1962 a Chinese PLA Division annihilated 7 Infantry Brigade in less than half a day. By midday there was no communication or information about units and formation. An eerie silence for 24 hours.

However, we, on the other axis of the Chinese advance, got to know from the first stragglers that our Battalion Adjutant Captain Mahavir Prasad (with the Field Rank of Major during the battle), summoned on special duty to 7 Brigade Headquarters, was killed in action, while manning an LMG in a 1/9 GR platoon locality. He was awarded the Mahavir Chakra for gallantry.

It was a great loss for the Battalion and a very personal loss for me. Mahavir was my senior, a mentor and personal friend. He was highly professional and was loved by the men. The question - what was Mahavir doing in the Namka Chu

area, two days march away from his battalion's AOR*? The author has covered Mahavir's role at Namka Chu in detail.

On the Bumla - Towang front, the Chinese attacked and cleared the AR** post at Bumla in the early hours of 23 October 1962. The Chinese advance was then effectively checked, first by a screen platoon at IB Ridge. Then later that day, at Tongpengla, our D Coy with a battery of mountain guns, blunted three assaults, gave the Chinese a bloody nose, caused many casualties and effectively halted their advance towards Towang.

But lo behold! To our great consternation, our Battalion was ordered to withdraw and fall back on Towang. No reason was forthcoming for that bizarre order. Rest is history. It is only later that we learnt the full extent and implications of 7 Brigade's rout on the left flank of the Towang front, and what it did to our whole 4 Division area of responsibility.

The author has been relentless and meticulous in piecing to-gether the truth, accounting for each ground reality of mili-tary activity, human travail, display of raw courage, privation of soldiers - in conditions created by the senior most leader- ship. This is an objective in-depth study and analysis of how and why the conflict came about. Also, it tells the story of the naivete of the political leadership in matters geopolitical. As also policy prevarications vis a vis China and the handling of the Indian armed forces. Ineptness of military leadership and freewheeling by politicized army generals in operational handling of units and formation, have been studied in detail.

This is a work dedicated to posterity. Generations to come must know the truth.

(signed)

Major General Krishen Khorana (Retd.) Panchkula

September 2022

Editor's notes-

AOR - Area of Responsibility. In this case of an army battalion.

AR - Assam Rifles, a para military organisation that was deployed at frontier posts in Nefa (North east frontier agency).

Preface

As a child, I was excited by war stories. One story in particular, disturbed me no end. My father, Amal Mukherjee, who was with Indian Airlines, used to tell me about his experiences while serving at, what was then - Dum Dum Airport, Calcutta, during the India - China war of 1962. He used to talk about his recollections of casualty-evacuation flights coming from Nefa (North east frontier agency) and "burly Sardars with their lower parts, waist downwards, completely 'melted', being carried off planes"! That was my first exposure to the horrors of war, albeit second hand.

I grew up with other war stories and subsequently researched World War-IL I wrote in international military-history sites. I actively posted on WW-II, in social media. Then one day, a friend on twitter, Conrad Barwa, asked me why was I not researching Indian military history!? That, over time, brought me to this book-project about those "burly Sardars", and others, who fought in that wretched war of 1962 in Nefa.

Enroute to this project, I wrote articles for the defense and strategic affairs website - India Sentinels and made videos under the Sandy Wars series, on their YouTube channel. This book is the culmination of all the encouragement and appreciation I received from Jayanta Bhattacharya, the Editor of India Sentinels and my mentors in the Indian defense-eco system.

Finally, my daughter, Shankhabela, literally pushed me into this book-project, to leave, in her words, something for posterity. Let us see how it goes.Kolkata, September 2022

Prologue

It was the morning of 20 October, 1962, Second Lieutenant A.J.S. Behl, Gun Position Officer, E troop, 17 Para Field regiment was in a trench on the Tsangdhar Ridge. His two artillery pieces, previously air dropped, were in position and firing over open sights into the thick of the Chinese assault all along the Namka Chu river. Other Indian troops, part of broken units and sub units were running back pell mell through his Gun Positions. Suddenly an officer from one of those groups jumped into his trench and asked him - "where is their firing coming from?" Behl indicated a feature to the left of Thag la (as seen from the south) on the ridge line, to the north, opposite Tsangdhar. The next moment one of those bullets came and hit the other officer in the head and he fell dead.

In war, one side usually wins and the other loses. That is the conventional wisdom. If viewed philosophically, at a human level, then mostly there are no real winners in war. However, where the agenda of nation-states are concerned, wars have outcome, success or failure.

India's 1962 war with China was a strange affair. It suddenly started and just as suddenly ended. And after it ended, the victorious side, voluntarily gave up a lot of the spoils of war. But men died, a lot of them actually. And many carried permanent disabilities and emotional scars. It was not just the futility of this war, but it's often bizarre conduct, on the Indian side, that stands out in the annals of military history! Seldom has an entire infantry brigade, along with its sup- porting arms, been so quickly routed and destroyed, as was the Indian 7 Infantry Brigade, at the Nama Chu front, in Nefa, in October 1962.

As I write this, we are at the threshold of the 60th anniversary of this epoch-making battle. Anniversaries come and go. But this year it will be different. On this anniversary, we will raise a toast to the real facts surrounding this national tragedy and banish the fiction.

Cheers!

Contents

Dedication V

Acknowledgements VI

Foreword IX

preface XIII

Prologue XV

What Is This Story All About? 1

The Political Backdrop; Nehru's Approach To China, His
Role In Military Affairs; The Matter Of Lt General "Biji" Kaul. 4

The Tortuous Path To Nam Ka Chu; Forward Policy; Mcmahon
Line And Bizarre Games Played Around It; Kaul Goes To War -
Operation Leghorn; Role Of Army Head Quarters; Defeat 18

The Hidden Key To Nam Ka Chu Mystery Of Captain Mahavir
Prasad's Patrol, His Report Ignored & A Historical Injustice
Done To Him; Mao Chooses War - The Casus Belli; Indian Army
Wobbles - 'Neither Cautious Legality Nor Pre-Emptive Boldness 52

20th October 1962,The Day Of Reckoning; The Chinese Plan And
Execution; Who Did What On The Indian Side; The Tales Of Glory
And Disgrace; At Whose Door Does The Shame Lie? 75

About The Author 99

What Is This Story All About?

Generations of Indians have grown up internalizing a standard narrative on the 1962 border war between India and China. India lost a huge chunk of its land to the Chinese that it had historically held, due to political ineptitude, interference and nepotism. And this was brought on by the unspeakable blunders of the-then prime minister, Jawaharlal Nehru, and his defence minister, Krishna Menon.

According to this narrative, some of their blunders included:

- Nehru's neglect of the Indian military. His weakness towards China and "appeasement of the Chinese".

- His preference for "incompetent sycophants", like Lieutenant General Brij Mohan Kaul, a fellow Kashmiri pandit, after ignoring "legendary professionals", like General Kodendera Subayya Thimmayya and his "rightful successor" Lieutenant General Shankarrao Pandurang Patil Thorat. Apart from Kaul, General Pran Nath Thapar, Brigadier DK "Monty" Palit and Lieutenant General Lionel Protip "Bogey" Sen were also supposed to be "incompetent officers" who were patronized by Nehru and Menon.

- The "suicidal" "Forward Policy", whereby Indian posts were pushed forward aggressively, with no tactical considerations (like the location of the Dho-la post), purely for the show of flag - a politicians' folly."

- The government's interference in purely military decisions that led to ultimate disaster.

- In this project, we have set out to examine each of these propositions, keeping aside opinions or predispositions, in the light of documented facts and events, rather than hearsay, innuendo and unsupported anecdotes.

Given the vast scope of the subject, we will limit our focus on the following:

The personality-based blame game.

- Documented policies, statements and memoirs related to the relevant policies, decisions, and pronouncements of that period.

- Military orders, instructions, reports, recommendations, and decisions.

- We have chosen the infamous Namka-chu debacle, in the Tawang sector of Nefa (now Arunachal Pradesh) for an exhaustive and objective analysis. For this, we have studied official documents, formally published or not, spoken to officers from the units involved, participants and experts. We have taken care to mostly include what is verifiable. To our knowledge, an exercise of this complexity and magnitude has never been attempted before, for this particular battle, outside the officially sponsored studies. This includes the debate about the relative merits of the Dho-la post vis a vis the much favoured location at Thag-la.

- Research work on various aspects of the India- China conflict and related matters by scholars.

Our scope of study and analysis will exclude the widely known and elaborately described combat narratives unless those have a direct bearing on the themes and focus of our study. There are, in fact, excellent published accounts from officers who have fought in those actions. The likes of, then 7 Brigade commander, Brigadier John Dalvi M1,

then CO of 4 Division Signals, Major General KK Tewari M2 and then Gun Position Officer (GPO), E Troop, 17 Para Field Regiment (deployed on Tsangdhar ridge) Brigadier AJ.S. Behl M3. Thus, we have only included those actions of the Namka chu battle which help us delve into the merits of the command process and commanders' attitude and conduct.

From left to right: Lt Col Rattan Singh, deputed to Assam Rifles,

commanding the Niyamjung chu sub sector, directly under HQ 4 Div., Lt Col BS Ahluwalia, CO 119 GR, Brig John Dalvi, commanding 7 brigade, Lt Col MS Rikh, CO 2 Rajput and Lt Col KK Tewari, CO 4 division-signals (Photo via claudearpi.net).

Therefore, if any reader wants to get a feel of what the actual action was like, in short a "war story", then no armchair analyst can bring them a better and truer feel than the above officers, who fought in it.

THE POLITICAL BACKDROP; NEHRU'S APPROACH TO CHINA, HIS ROLE IN MILITARY AFFAIRS; THE MATTER OF LT GENERAL "BIJI" KAUL.

Was Nehru and the Indian leadership 'soft' on China?

Let us give a wide berth to Indian political lore and partisan commentaries on this subject and look at the facts as presented by international scholars.

Our reading is that the Chinese, and particularly Chinese chairman, Mao Zedong, himself, were always deeply suspicious of Nehru personally due to his elite - "class" background. To doctrinaire Marxists, the "class" aspect is the fundamental prism through which the world is viewed. Nehru was considered a "reactionary" dictated to by the Indian and western, big bourgeoisie. All his actions, attitudes and pronouncements on Tibet and China were viewed through this filter. Finally, the real motivation for the war, was the conviction among Chairman Mao and the Chinese leadership that Nehru had designs on Tibet [R1].

Nehru viewed China as a huge landmass of fellow Asians, which had been tormented and exploited for long by imperialists. Hence, he perceived a commonality of interest between India and China in the early days. However, from 1949 onwards his perspective on China was pragmatic rather than "sentimental". The way he saw it, the People's Republic of China, as a large neighbor, wasn't going any place else. They are here to stay, and we might as well accept them and coexist on a friendly basis, to mutual benefit.

Taiwan was a tiny footnote to the Chinese story in real terms, irrespective of the ideological intransigence of the US over the issue. All the talk of "Hindi-Chini Bhai Bhai" India-China are brothers) is akin to the "biryani and hugging" bonhomie one has seen with our western neighbour from time to time, but practiced on a larger, institutional scale.

On Tibet, Nehru knew and understood the legacy of China's suzerainty over Tibet since ancient times. He also recognized the reality of Tibet's autonomous and special status within the larger reality of China's sovereign rights. He tried to marry India's special historical and "sentimental" relationship with Tibet with the "special and autonomous" aspect of Tibet's status within the People's Republic of China.

John Garver quoting from Claude Arpi and Tsering Shakya, encapsulates Nehru's approach succinctly [R2]

"Nehru envisioned a compromise between Chinese and Indian interests regarding Tibet, with Chinese respect for Tibetan autonomy combined with Indian respect for Chinese sovereignty over Tibet. This accommodation would, Nehru believed, provide a basis for a broad program of cooperation between China and India on be- half of the peoples of the developing countries and against the insanity of a nuclear-armed bipolar Cold War. Nehru believed that by demonstrating India s acceptance of China's ownership and military control of Tibet while simultaneously befriending China on such is- sues as war in Korea, the PRCs UN admission, the peace treaty with Japan and transfer of Taiwan to the PRC, Indochina, and decolonization and the Afro-Asian movement, China could be won to co- operation with India. The two leading Asian powers would then create a new axis in world politics. In terms of Tibet, Nehru hoped that China would repay India's friendship and consolidate the Sino- Indian partnership by granting Tibet a significant degree of autonomy."

However, China's increasing interference in and coercive impositions on Tibet disappointed Nehru deeply. This is where his schism with the Chinese Communist Party leadership began. And China's later distrust and paranoia over the border issue, emanated from their leadership's deep resentment over Nehru's stance on Tibet. Mao read Nehru's intentions towards Tibet as the quest for a buffer state between India and China. He saw Nehru's actions through the pedantic Marxist paradigm of class sympathy for the "serf owning oppressors" of the Dalai Lama's genre.

The Chinese leadership was infuriated that Nehru was apparently not recognizing China's absolute suzerainty over Tibet. According to them, Nehru was continuously diluting

China's authority in Tibet through all the talk of autonomy and special status. Apart from Nehru's purported actions in encouraging reactionary and "anti-progressive" sections of Tibet's Buddhist theocracy.

Ironically the-then Chinese premier, Zhou En Lai, had previously agreed with Nehru on the historically autonomous legacy of Tibet within the PRC.

Resistance fighters on the Tibetan border during the early years of the CIA.'s Tibet program. (Photo courtesy: Lhamo Tsering's collection.)

To this was added the aspect of the Tibetan insurgency and India's role in it. For all the talk of passive and non-violent Tibetan resistance, which was publicly professed by Nehru, he was in the know about, and condoned, the United States' Central Intelligence Agency's campaign of subversion and armed insurrection in Tibet. Here, the Indian intelligence agencies covered its tracks very well. In period pieces, written around that time, no author or analyst could prove India's role in armed Tibetan resistance. However, research into CIA's archives and sources R3 shows that the Indian intelligence agencies supported the CIA's efforts actively.

Did Nehru neglect the Indian military?

Yes, the Indian armed forces were much weaker in the first decade after independence, than they are now. The country was just getting on its feet after the widespread bloodshed and displacement that happened during Partition and the first Kashmir war. The new republic was plagued with a plethora of socio-economic problems as a colonial legacy. Indigenous capital formation was low. There was a multitude of vital sectors crying for investment and outlay of funds. Big powers were lying in wait to incorporate India into the armed camps of the Cold War. Under those circum-stances, the leadership made a choice favouring peaceful na-tion building.

India's defence spending was low until 1960, as the below graph illustrates, both in absolute terms as well as with respect to GDP. India was surrounded by neighbours, poor and unsettled, as we were. Any serious military threat that could go beyond border clashes, was not on the radar. However Pakistani scholars have accused Nehru of using military threats even then, in the lead up to the Nehru - Liaquat Pact of April 1950.

1962 (when the Forward Policy was in place), as the graph below shows, changed all that. Nehru's defence budget for 1962 was 2.75% of GDP, a steep and sudden jump.

Just for the context, India's defence budget as a % (percentage) of GDP for 2018-19, 19-20, 20-21 have been 2.16, 2.2,2.4 and 2.16 respectively. Current fiscal's figure standing at 2.03% (as per budget documents).

For additional perspective, in the 3rd Plan (1961-66), the total allocation for the health sector was 2.9% of the total planned expenditure. India was a poor, newly independent, and a "third world" nation then. Therefore, it is questionable whether Nehru's India "neglected" its military, given the context.

Equally important is, how did we use and leverage those modest funds allocated to defence, ever since the borders with China became troublesome? Analysing this, we would, sadly, find that Nehru expected much more from the military than what he could invest in it - for many years. The impact of years of low spending cannot be put right in a year (vis a vis the spike in budgetary allocation to defence in 62). So, it is not wrong to say that the initial inability on his part, to engage with realpolitik, partly contributed to the constraints that the military faced vis a vis the border conflict. And this personal failing perhaps aggravated the emotional shock (due to the military debacle) that he suffered, towards the end of his life and career.

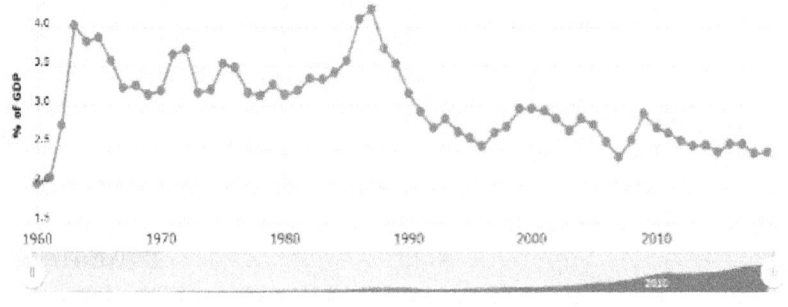

Data Source: World Bank

Deliberate preference for incompetent 'sycophants' at the cost of 'competent' officers?

A lot has been said and written about the quality of India's military leadership in this period. A popular narrative is that "competent" officers were left out and mediocre people were deliberately appointed in key leadership positions. Let us study this proposition in brief and take a look at the background and military credentials of the officers involved in this game of "deserving vs favourites".

Lieutenant General **Shankarrao Pandurang Patil** (SPP) *Thorat*, KC, DSO, the officer who is said to have been the right choice as General Thimmayya's successor as COAS (Chief Of Army Staff) [F1], passed from the Royal Military College, Sandhurst in August 1926. He did his stint in the Staff College, Quetta. He saw extensive combat against the Japanese, first in the Naga Hills and Imphal sector and then in the re-conquest of Burma.

After arriving at the front in 1944 and getting temporary command of a unit (9/14 Punjab), Thorat faced raised eyebrows from Brigadier DAL Mackenzie for personally accompanying the rifle companies on a long recce mission. Again, in Burma's Kangaw sector, in January 1945, this time as CO of 2/2 Punjab, after taking heavy casualties in a frontal attack, the 39-year-old Thorat joined his forward troops in hand-to-hand combat at Hill-170, snatched the sword of a much younger Japanese officer and slayed him on the way up.

Lt Col SPP Thorat, CO of 2nd Punjab Battalion, comes down from hill captured by his men after bitter fight.

(Photo courtesy Dr. YSP Thorat, son of Lt Gen SPP Thorat.)

And what about the "sycophant" officers who get com- pared to him, like Thapar, who was made the Army chief instead of Thorat and the Eastern Army (Eastern Command) commander Sen?

General PN Thapar, Chief of Army Staff (Photo from the album of Ranjit Sahgal).

General Pran Nath Thapar, PVSM, the much-maligned Army chief to actually succeed General Thimmayya, was also an alumnus of Sandhurst, who passed out from the prestigious military academy in February 1926, as the latter's batchmate. And in addition to Staff College, Quetta, he had attended the true-blue senior Staff College, Camberley too.

Gen Thapar was a Brigade Major with the 8th Army in the Middle East and Italy in the World War II, along with other staff positions, "managing" combat forces in battle, which included British units in the brigade. As an Indian, how much more military "glamour" do you want in the British Indian Army?

If you grind on the "effectiveness" and "combat record" over seniority, then how about General (later Field Marshal) Sam Hormusji Framji Jamshedji Manekshaw becoming the Army chief in 1969, based on "seniority", rather than Lieutenant General Harbaksh Singh, the war hero of Tithwal (who won his Vir Chakra in the 1948 war in Kashmir), and the "saviour" of Punjab in the India-Pakistan war of 1965? Sam won the 1971 war. But who knew that in 1969?

Now let's come to *Lieutenant General* **Lionel Protip "Bogey"** *Sen,* DSO, the much-talked-about commander of the Eastern Army in 1962. He too was commissioned from Sandhurst, in August 1931. **He** too served in the 51 Indian Infantry Brigade in Burma (as CO of 16/10 Baloch) along with Thimmayya and Thorat. Incidentally, this brigade was nicknamed the "Indian Brigade" since all its three battalions were Indian and commanded by Indian officers (Thimmayya, Thorat and Sen).

This was unique in the British Indian Army where the brigades had two Indian units with the third being British. And even the Indian battalions were mostly commanded by British officers. Coincidentally, all three of these Indian officers were awarded the DSO (Distinguished Service Order) for actions in the same area at the same time (Burma's Arakan, near Kangaw, where, among other things, the famous battle for Hill 170, code named "MELROSE", took place in January 1945.

> **The Distinguished Service Order**
> Brigadier (temporary) Derek Jarrett STEEVENS, C.B.E., M.C. (5389), late Royal Regiment of Artillery.
> Lieutenant-Colonel (temporary) Richard John UNIAKE (41184), Royal Regiment of Artillery (London, S.W.3).
> Lieutenant-Colonel (temporary) Bernard Archibald SHATTOCK (69954), The Queen's Royal Regiment (West Surrey) (Dormans Land, Surrey).
> Lieutenant-Colonel (temporary) Theodore Henry BIRBECK (44960), The Border Regiment (attached The King's African Rifles).
> Lieutenant-Colonel (acting) Philip Turner van STRAUBENZEE (53744), The Oxfordshire and Buckinghamshire Light Infantry) (attached The Sierra Leone Regiment) (Layburn, Yorks.).
> Major (temporary) Edward Oliver Whitaker HUNT (EC.188057), General List (Malvern Wells).
> Lieutenant-Colonel (acting) Lionel Protip SEN (IA.77), 10th Baluch Regiment, Indian Army.
> Lieutenant-Colonel (acting) Shankarrao Pandurang Patil THORAT (IA.536), 14th Punjab Regiment, Indian Army.
> Lieutenant-Colonel (temporary) Kodandera Subayya THIMAYYA (IA.944), 19th Hyderabad Regiment, Indian Army.

Supplement to the London Gazette, November 15, 1945.

Sen won further laurels after Independence while commanding the 161 Brigade in the Kashmir valley, in the first India-Pakistan War. Remember those halcyon days of late 1947 when the fate of Jammu & Kashmir hung by a "slender thread" (in his own words)?

Lt General LP Sen (Photo credit: Unknown photographer)

For Sen, it was Hill 170 all over again, but on a larger scale. He arrived during a command crisis. Lieutenant Colonel Dewan Ranjit Rai, CO of 1 Sikh (the first unit to arrive at Kashmir) had been killed in action, on October 28, the day after his arrival. Brigadier JC Katoch, commander of 161 Brigade, had been injured and evacuated on November 1, 1948. That was when Sen was summoned by the commander in chief of the Indian Army, General Sir Rob Lockhart, promoted as an acting Brigadier and ordered to fly to Srinagar and take over the brigade next morning.

Such was the rush that Sen borrowed the additional shoulder pips required for a brigadier's uniform, from a staff officer and went to meet Lieutenant General Dudley Russell, the commander of the Delhi and East Punjab Command, for his briefing.

The British officer was frank and to the point. During his briefing of Sen, Russel said: "I am not allowed to enter the (Kashmir) valley. You will have to find your way about when you get there." The way Sen's brigade fetched up in record time and pushed back the barbaric tribal militiamen from the doorsteps of Srinagar has remained an understated achievement in the annals of military history.

161 Brigade after arriving in Srinagar (Photo credit: Indian Army).

As an aside, since this article aims to dispel certain myths about the Indian military's history, Sen received very "martial" and no-nonsense advice and blessings from two unlikely quarters before proceeding to his command.

Cursing Mahatma Gandhi, for his pacifism and "weakness" for the enemy, is favourite pastime of the Indian myth-making circles. On the same evening when he was given his promotion and his mission, Sen met Gandhi for his blessings. This is what Bapu told him: "Wars are a curse to humanity; they bring nothing but suffering and destruction. You're going in to protect innocent people, and to save them from suffering and their property from destruction. To achieve that you must naturally make full use of every means at your disposal."

The moral basis for India's intervention in Kashmir couldn't be better summed up than these words from a "pacifist".

Similarly, the role of the British officers in the subcontinent has been severely castigated and dubbed "anti-India" during the J&K crisis. At the political level, the departing Raj admittedly played a shady role and some of their officers (like the ones with the Gilgit Scouts) played a dirty game. But Russell's parting words to Sen couldn't have been clearer and professional. He said, "The only advice that I can give you is that if you get a chance of hitting them, hit hard with all you have got and don't let up."

Who and what was Lt General B.M. Kaul?

And now we come to an officer who is the "villain of the piece" for many. The officer who is said to have almost singlehandedly caused the disaster in the North-East Frontier Agency (Nefa) - the redoubtable Lieutenant General Brij Mohan Kaul, PVSM.

There are allegations of favouritism because of his being Nehru's Kashmiri Brahmin kin and Menon's "favourite". He was made the GOC of IV Corps (the formation that fought in Kameng - in the Namka-chu/Dho-la Post fiasco) just before the war. This corps was carved out of the XXX Corps which was hitherto looking after the entire region.

He is accused of many things.

Firstly, he was not from the combat arms, being an ASC (Army Supply Corps) officer. He was into politicking and in-fluence peddling. Since he had the ear of Nehru and Menon, he wielded influence disproportionate to his position, that is, his superiors in the Army were deferential to him. As per this narrative, he was accommodated as GOC, IV Corps, in the Kameng sector since he supported the "asinine" Forward Policy and its inevitable denouement - the border war with China. And in that role, he was a disaster - directly responsible for the mayhem at Namka-chu.

Some say he was a coward and shirker too when the chips were down for "falling ill" while in the forward position, just before the action started and had to be evacuated to a Delhi hospital. Where he (conveniently) sat out the battle in his hospital bed. In short, he is the perfect fall guy to carry all the blame, for the debacle in Nefa.

Interestingly this is what the dailymail.com.uk had to say about Lt General Kaul and the other Indian dramatis personae of the 1962 war, in 2014, after the Henderson Brooks report was leaked on the internet.

So before coming to Kaul's role in the disaster at Namka-chuthe scene of the first episode in this tragedy - let us objectively scan his military record till then, sans the political commentary.

Kaul also passed out from Sandhurst. Over the years, after Independence, he became a kind of a "go-to man" for the Indian government, where special military situations were concerned. Kaul was always painfully aware that he hadn't seen combat. And like many people with martial ambitions, without formal opportunities to make their bones in action, he went out of his way to seek out adventure and perilous situations. This, as we shall see, led to shallowness in faculties essential for a general staff officer, like operational appreciation in depth. His style and penchant throughout remained that of a swashbuckling, go-to man, seeking instant thrills.

During the Liberation of Goa, in December 1961, Kaul, then the CGS, with no call to physically participate in com- bat, insisted on joining the forward troops of 63 Brigade spearheading Operation Vijay. Accordingly, as soon as 3 Sikh crossed the border at 5.15am on December 17, on the "Yellow Route" en-route Mollem, Kaul followed suit, in the company of Brigadier KS Dhillon.

This act of bravado was unnecessary for a chief of general staff and unheard of. His skills and presence were not relevant to front line combat operations here!

By the way, as the CGS of the Indian Army, Kaul's planning and handling of logistics for this operation, were brilliant and execution superb.

However, his bravado and courage were not always mis- directed. The year before Operation Vijay, he was assigned by Nehru and Menon to go and sort out a tricky situation in Nagaland. An IAF Dakota on a supply run to the isolated post at Purr, had been shot down by Naga insurgents and its crew taken captive. Kaul landed by helicopter in the insurgents' territory with a rescue team and successfully retrieved the captives. Again, this was not, strictly speaking, a CGS's job. Nonetheless, it was very impressive to behold.

THE TORTUOUS PATH TO NAM KA CHU; FORWARD POLICY; MCMAHON LINE AND BIZARRE GAMES PLAYED AROUND IT; KAUL GOES TO WAR - OPERATION LEGHORN; ROLE OF ARMY HEAD QUARTERS; DEFEAT

Namka-chu valley - the ' crime Scene'; Kaul goes to war.

The 26 km Namka Chu (Kejielang in Chinese) river valley, as seen from above the tri junction of Bhutan - Tibet and India.

This story focuses on the circumstances and reasons be- hind India's military defeat in the western subsector (Kameng Frontier Division) of Nefa in the infamous battle of Namka-chu. The virtual destruction of Brig John Dalvi's 7 Brigade (under Parshad's 4 Division), in a few hours, is the most ignominious chapter in the military history of Independent India. However, like we said at the beginning, we would not get into the widely known details of the actual battle, which are easily available in published form, written by direct participants in that tragedy.

So let us begin by examining Kaul's actual actions as GOC of IV Corps, in October 1962. The sequence, timing, sub- stance, and impact of those actions [R4].

Kaul, then the CGS (Chief of General Staff), was called back from leave on October 3, 1962 and informed about his new appointment as General Officer commanding of IV Corps, by Thapar, the Army chief, at 9 pm at the latter's residence. He flew to Tezpur next day (October 4) and arrived in the afternoon. There he had a conference with Sen, who was the Eastern Army commander then, Lieutenant General Umrao Singh, GOC of XXXIII Corps (the new IV Corps command was carved out of the XXXIII Corps area).

The briefing Kaul received from his predecessor impressed him enough to promptly send a signal to the Eastern Army (whose commander he had just met) and Thapar that the Chinese intended to ambush the Indian Army in the Dhola-Tsangdhar sector with the intention of capturing Tawang.

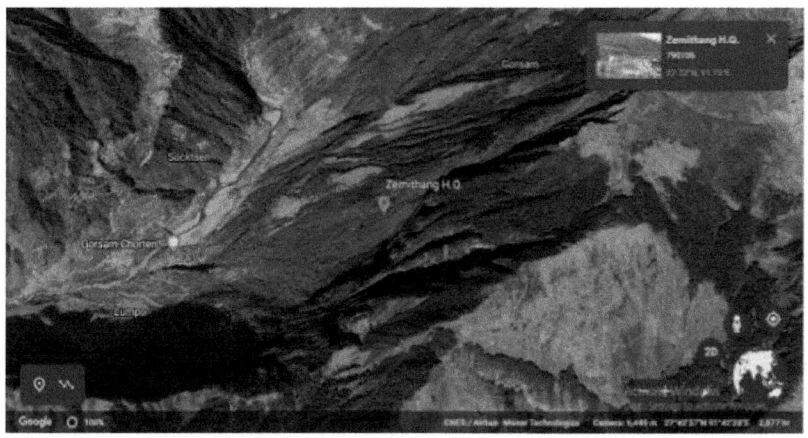

The Zemithang base area, with helicopter landing ground and HQs

On October 5, 1962, Kaul flew to Darranga airstrip and took a helicopter to Zemithang ALG (advanced landing ground). There, he was briefed by a field intelligence asset about the ground situation and the Chinese strength. Kaul sent a signal to Eastern Command and AHQ to the effect:

- That the Chinese had at least a brigade concentrated in the Thag-la area already.
- The Chinese weapons in this area included artillery, heavy mortars, and recoilless guns.
- He could not (in view of our lean and their far superior resources) rule out the possibility of the enemy overwhelming our forces.
- Unless we retrieved this situation speedily, we might have a national disaster.
- Therefore, he recommended, as a precautionary measure, offensive air support to be positioned suitably without delay and made available to him at the shortest notice, if necessary.

(a) Enemy had strengthened his position and was supported not only by artillery and heavy mortars but had other "dangerous weapons such as RCL guns and automatic rifles".

TOP SECRET

(b) He was convinced that the enemy had in addition to their forward battalion, a brigade in close support in the THAGLA Area.

(c) He was, therefore, accelerating the concentration of troops by every means and also taking steps to "outwit the enemy and capture our objectives". Operations would, in any case, start on 10 October.

(d) The enemy overwhelming our troops, however, could not be ruled out. The stakes were high and, in order to speedily retrieve the situation, offensive air support must be planned and positioned.

From the Henderson Brooks Report - hitherto referred to as HBR [R5]

Regardless of what Kaul had done in the past, the dates and contents of Kaul's signals to higher command, at this point in time, are noteworthy. Do we see, at this stage of the unfolding events, an officer blind to reality and misleading his superiors about the equation on the ground, as some have insinuated?

No.

Then again, this same officer, in his earlier avatar as CGS, had been deeply involved with the policies and decisions that led to the mess, which he now found himself in. It is important to note this nuance, in order to affix command responsibility for whatever happened later.

Kaul's general staff's opinions and appreciation of the strategic and operational situation, at that stage, is succinctly conveyed through a comment made by his officiating CGS, Major General JS Dhillon, a month earlier, in September, when he was on leave. Maj Gen Dhillon told the Eastern Army commander, L.P. Sen: "Experience in Ladakh had shown that a few rounds fired at the Chinese would cause them to run away." (This was quoted in the official history of the 1962 war).

Therefore, how does the reader evaluate Kaul's predicament? An essentially "go to" adventurer had been given the job of CGS (with political leanings factored in by the defence minister), which requires a very different set of aptitudes? That apart, what did Army Headquarters (AHQ) do about his signals which warned about dire consequences and a cataclysmic military outcome?

Some pointers to both these rhetorical questions lie in the curious goings on at AHQ, both at command and staff levels, in this one year, that led the Indian Army by the hand, to this situation at Namka-chu.

The (in)famous "Forward Policy.

Nehru's government gave a policy decision on the Chinese frontier issue, the much talked about "Forward Policy", on November 2, 1961. From the Army's side, the chief, General Thapar, was present. Given below is the operative part of the policy as laid out by the government. There are no records to establish whether Thapar presented his own AHQ's annual intelligence review on China-Tibet, in 1959-60, which clearly stated that China's People Liberation occupied by it. Point C of the policy, as can be see below, ap- pears to have catered to the risk of confrontation. Therefore, the Army's apprehensions may have been factored in.

> "(a) So far as LADAKH is concerned, we are to patrol as far forward as possible from our present positions towards the International border. This will be done with a view to establishing our posts which should prevent the Chinese from advancing further and also dominating from any posts which they may have already established in our territory. This must be done without getting involved in a clash with the Chinese, unless this becomes necessary in self defence.
>
> (b) As regards UP and other Northern areas, there are not the same difficulties as in LADAKH. We should, therefore, as far as practicable, go forward and be in effective occupation of the whole frontier. Where there are any gaps, they must be covered either by patrolling or by posts.
>
> (c) In view of numerous operational and administrative difficulties, efforts should be made to position major concentration of forces along our borders in places conveniently situated behind the forward posts from where they could be maintained logistically and from where they can restore a border situation at short notice."

HBR

About the intent behind this Forward Policy, the **Official History Of The 1962 War** [R6] (hitherto referred to as the **Official History**), informs us as under:

> 88. According to Neville Maxwell, it was B.N. Mullik who argued that the Chinese intended to come right up to their claim line but that they would keep away where Indian troops were present even if in a small number and hence the Indian Army should quickly move forward to fill the vacuum, as otherwise Chinese were bound to do so within a few months. The final outcome of that meeting was on the lines suggested by him. India's China War, p.221. According to Lt Gen B.M. Kaul, who was also present in that meeting, Nehru framed this policy principally for the benefit of the Parliament and pubic and also perhaps as a 'strategy of beating the Chinese at their own game'. The Untold Story (New Delhi, 1967) p.281.

While Neville Maxwell, according to us, is a prejudiced source, this particular aspect appears to have been corroborated by the then CGS and even otherwise makes sense.

The Forward Policy, which was primarily meant for Ladakh, has been made out to be an irresponsible and frivo- lous stupidity, in the plethora of ill-informed narratives that have been widely published and circulated, since 1962. However, this document seems to be a cautious and balanced attempt to restore India's rights of sovereignty over alienated chunks of territory, while being mindful of the military unc-

ertainty inherent in such ventures. The Forward Policy's application in Nefa's, Kameng Frontier Division, has a different nuance vis a vis the situation in Ladakh. We shall examine that later in this story. What is astounding is the action that AHQ (Army Head Quarters) took, or rather didn't take, while

> "1 The policy regarding patrolling and establishing posts with reference to INDO-TIBET Border has recently been reviewed by Government. The decisions taken by Government are reflected in the succeeding paragraphs.
>
> **LADAKH**
>
> 2 We are to patrol as far forward as possible from our present positions towards the International Border as recognised by us. This will be done with a view to establishing additional posts located to prevent the Chinese from advancing further and also to dominate any Chinese posts already established in our territory.
>
> 3 This "Forward Policy" shall be carried out without getting involved in a clash with the Chinese unless it becomes necessary in self-defence.
>
> **UP and other Northern borders**
>
> 4 As regards UP and other Northern areas, there are not the same difficulties as in LADAKH. We should, therefore, as far as practicable, go forward and be in effective occupation of the whole frontier. Gaps should be covered either by patrolling or by posts.
>
> **Reappraisal of tasks**
>
> 5 I realise that the application of this new policy in LADAKH and on our other borders will entail considerable movements of troops with attendant logistical problems. I would like you to make a fresh appraisal of your task in view of the new directive from Government, especially with regard to the additional logistical effort involved. Your recommendations in this respect are required by me by 30 December, 1961. Meanwhile, wherever possible, action should be taken as indicated above."

operationalizing this Forward Policy. After no visible action was taken for a month after the above meeting, thereby losing precious time, AHQ released the following order, according to the **Henderson Brooks Report (HBR):**

Conspicuous by its absence is the critical "Point C" of GOI's original Forward Policy document issued on November 2! The AHQ, here makes no mention of any firm bases behind the forward posts, which would serve as logistic hubs and operational bases for the "major concentration of forces", which were essential pre-requisites for operationalizing the original policy.

Therefore, as we can see, the AHQ is accountable for not only the emasculation of the military aspect of the Forward Policy but also for curious defiance against a policy directive from the highest level. Thus, the basic character of the

Forward Policy was changed in the processof its operationalisation.

It is obvious that Kaul's General Staff was fully involved in the above goings on and had helped push forward the 'penny packets' which constituted Army's advanced posts without doing anything about the essential prerequisite, like the operational and logistic bases envisioned by the government.

Now let us see what Kaul did, when he himself landed in the mess that he had helped create.

On October 6, Kaul reached the Army's forward positions at Bridge I (MM9114) in the Namka-chu ("chu" means "river" in Tibetan) valley, across which the Chinese held their positions. He was the first Indian general to have reached this forward defended locality (FDL). The local divisional commander (GOC, 4 Division), Major General Niranjan Parshad accompanied him. This means, no one in the command hierarchy, above a brigadier, had any first-hand feel about this area, which had assumed such criticality in the rapidly deteriorating India-China relationship.

Readers should note, in this context, that the entire Chinese frontier had been handed over to the Indian Army, after the violent confrontation in August 1959, at the Longju Post in Nefa. The first Indian Army unit, in history, to set foot in the Namka chu valley was 9 Punjab, under Lt. Colonel RN. Misra, on 14-15 September 1962, as given in the **Official History,** as under:

> CO 9 Punjab with Bn column left Lumpo for Dhola on 14 September. 'A' Coy was left at Bridge 1 on 15 September and 'B' and 'C' Coys were left at Bridge 2 on the Namkha Chu river. CO alongwith 'D' Coy moved forward to Dhola Post. He left 'D' Coy under Maj Chaudhary at Dhola and returned to Bridge 2 at 'B' and 'C' Coy's position(105).

However, the first Indian Army officer to go there was Captain Mahavir Prasad, in May 1962, whose story has been discussed in details later.

During his sojourn in the Namka chu-Dhola Post area (details of this post and the operational zone it covered, given later) between October 6 and 10, Kaul sent a series of signals to AHQ and Eastern Command ...

- On 7 October Kaul signaled AHQ and Eastern Army that (among other things) the bulk of the air-dropped supplies were landing in inaccessible places from where they couldn't be retrieved.

- 2 Rajput and 1/9 Gorkha had supplies for just 3 days, with 50 rounds of rifle ammo per man, mortars and ammunition being in transit from Lumpu (MM8906). Due to better resources, the Chinese were subsequently, likely to dislodge IA from any positions that may be gained initially.

However, Kaul, in his published version of the debacle, has nothing to say about the following findings given in the **HBR**

> 30. The difficulties were no doubt great and commendable work was done to try and overcome them. The shortage of some 1000 x 1-ton vehicles and 9000 pioneers reflects on the enormity of the logistical problem. It was precisely for these reasons that XXXIII Corps and 4 Infantry Division had insisted on prior stocking of DHOLA before the operations could be undertaken. It was height of bad planning and staff work to launch an operation and then mourn the shortfall in resources.
>
> 31. The meeting of the demand of 1200 x 1-ton vehicles and 9000 pioneers overnight by any army, let alone ours, is out of the question. It must be remembered that the initiative for mounting the operation was till then ours. It was, therefore, all the more possible and, of course, essential in that difficult country and extreme climate that the tactical plan was based on the available resources. What, however, was done was completely out of context with the realities of the situation. There is no doubt that General KAUL's ordering of 7 Infantry Brigade to DHOLA Area for operations, despite being fully briefed regarding the grave logistical shortcomings, can at best only be described as wanton disregard of the elementary principles of war.

So, for all his expressions of "incredulity in distress", after reaching Namka chu, Kaul knew much in advance, what he was getting 4 division into, in this sub sector. If he didn't, then he was a military nincompoop [F2]. And then on the 8th and 9th of October, Kaul suddenly changed track and his bluster returned! According to **HBR,** on the 8th he informed AHQ, of his implied tactical success as 9 Punjab sent a force up into the heights north of Namka chu.

> 44. The Corps Commander commenced preliminary operations by occupying SINGJANG with two platoons of which one section was at KARPOLA on 8 October 1962. The Chinese for sometime before this had made it quite clear by shouting and throwing messages that the Indians should not cross the NAMKA CHU. They had not reacted at TSANGLE, which was a considerable distance and at a flank from their defences at THAGLA Ridge. Another reason might well be that TSANGLE, according to the old maps, was in BHUTAN. The occupation of SINGJANG without opposition was notified to Army Headquarters by a signal from the Corps Commander on 8 October 1962. (Annexure 81). This

HBR

His intellectual disingenuousness in this matter is evident from his surprising attempt to paint a rosy picture of the situation on the 9th. He drafted a signal for AHQ, giving a glowing, self-congratulatory account of his supposed achievements which had turned the situation around! Gone was the candour of his earlier series of alarming signals to AHQ, the moment he sniffed an opportunity for self- projection. A shallow, self-serving person, superficially reacting to situations!

> 45. The Chinese as in the case of TSANGLE did not react immediately at SINGJANG. On 9 October, when there was still no reaction, the Corps Commander considered he had by bold action achieved a major success. He drafted a lengthy signal in the evening which indicated that by vigorous actions, numerous regroupings and introducing element of surprise he had reduced the disadvantage of his relative weakness. He had given a talk to officers and JCOs and found their morale high. He had found the troops willing to undertake any operations despite the handicaps and he had assured them he would remain with them.
>
> 46. The signal was, however, premature. On morning of 10 October the Chinese reacted vigorously and we were evicted from SINGJANG and KARPOLA. The signal was, therefore, not sent, but the filed manuscript copy indicated the Corps Commander's optimism on 9 October 1962. (Annexure 82).

HBR

Operation Leghorn of 10 October 1962 – the betrayal of Major M.S. Chaudhary and his men.

> "OP LEGHORN (.) ref conversation COAS/GOCINC of date(.) 9 PUNJAB as soon as possible after arr in DHOLA area will (.) alfa (.) capture the Chinese post 1000 yards north east of DHOLA post (.) bravo (.) contain Chinese cone south THAGLA (.) charlie (.) if possible est post KARPOLA MM 8220 and YUMTSO LA MM 8320 pass."

Operational order for Leghorn as quoted in HBR. For perspective it should be noted that the actual walking distance from the Dhola post to Thag-la atop the opposite ridge, was 9 miles

Let us now look at the content and tone of Kaul's signal to AHQ and Eastern command on 10 October, after the morn-ing battle at Tseng Jong (Operation Leghorn), where the aforementioned force from 9 Punjab (one platoon each from A and D companies, under Major M.S. Chaudhary) was overwhelmed by a Chinese battalion. This day, amidst the cold, dank jungles, tracks and rock faces of the Namka chu valley and overlooking heights, came Lt General Kaul's moment of truth. The Service Corps officer and subsequent 'paper pusher' in the General Staff, finally had a ring side view in a combat theatre.

Kaul informed his superiors that a grave situation had developed, post the action at Tseng Jong, the PLA had deployed a division against the 7 Brigade and the threat to Tawang it-self was now real. He suggested that he be allowed to visit AHQ in person for briefing and consultation at length. He believed that a wrong position had been chosen to fight. He had failed to arrange for supplies and logistic build up in time.

The problems were deep seated and would persist. Thus, the whole campaign should be revisited

So, what happened on the 10th that put a spanner in Kaul's euphoric state evidenced on the 9th? This attack was supposed to be the opening gambit of an ambitious opera tion (Operation Leghorn) to dislodge the PLA from Thag-la MM8717 (which India now resolved to claim assertively as her own territory as per the "Watershed Principle", seeking to re define the McMahon Line) and occupy it. The Chinese repeatedly attacked Maj Chaudhary's force from the east and the west with a full battalion supported by heavy weapons. The 9 Punjab men, being the first to arrive in that sector weeks ago, were acclimatized and familiar with the terrain. They held off a much superior enemy, over twelve times their number, through repeated assaults.

Major Chaudhary requested for the previously promised MMG and mortar support when the going got difficult. Brigadier Dalvi refused! Kaul denies, on record, any role in that refusal. Others claim he was consulted.

> 49   At about 0730 hours a battalion worth of Chinese emerged from their positions on the THAGLA Ridge and charged down towards Bridge 4. Some 800 yards above the NAMKA CHU, they wheeled RIGHT towards SINGJANG. It was at this time that Major CHAUDHRI, the Officer at SINGJANG, asked for support from MMG Commander at Bridge 4. Two requests were made for MMG and Mortar support to the JCO in charge. The JCO asked permission to open up from the Brigade Commander, who with the Divisional and Corps Commander were at an OP (Observation Post) nearby. The Brigade Commander, after consultation with the Corps Commander refused permission. The JCO after the second request persisted and even went to the extent to suggest that the Corps Commander's party could move away in case the Chinese retaliated on the MMG Post, when the latter opened up. The JCO was convinced that with the ammunition available he could have broken up the attack. The permission, however, was still not granted. (Statement of MMG JCO - Annexure 83 - and Statement by Brig MR RAJWADE, MC - Annexure 84).

HBR

Kaul says that Dalvi's reason for refusal were:

- The battle zone was perhaps out of range for the MMG and mortars.
- There wasn't sufficient ammunition.
- The Chinese would bring down retaliatory fire on the 2 Rajput positions at Bridge N.

The Official History of the battle quotes Jemadar Mohan Lal, the MMG platoon JCO as insisting that he has sufficient ammunition (12000 rounds) and could mow down the Chinese troops, advancing across his line of sight.

> According to Jem Mohan Lal, the Senior Commanders' reason for not allowing gun support for the Tseng-jong platoon was that it would give the Chinese excuse to fire on Bridge IV and that there was not sufficient ammunition with the MMGs. But, as regards the availability of ammunition, Jem Mohan Lal had informed them that he had 12000 rounds with him and that was sufficient to break up the Chinese attack. He was expected to receive fresh supply of ammunition, the next day. He, in fact, received 22,000 rounds, as expected.
>
> Jem Mohan Lal was confident that if he had been allowed to fire, he could well have prevented the attack as there was little cover available for the Chinese, and they would have all the time been enfiladed to his guns.

Official History

Kaul's description of the scene in front of him, as the battle started, paints a surprising picture any standards. Apparently 2 Rajput's men were moving willy nilly, in the open, towards the log bridges over Namka chu, for crossing over towards the northern heights that led up to Tseng Jong and Thag-la. Brigadier Dalvi had incredibly chosen not to get the men across under cover of darkness, the previous night and ordered this deployment in daylight, in full view of the enemy sitting on commanding heights (on the night of 19th October, the Chinese infiltrated through the same area, at night, in the opposite direction, and got behind the Indian positions). Thus, Dalvi feared that what Mohan Lal could do to the enemy on the northern slopes, the Chinese in turn could do to the Indians.

Our readers can perhaps now assess how a motivated, brave force, had its morale busted and confidence in com- mand negated through this strange style and tactics at the Brigade level! How an inept, timid commander, set the tone for 7 Brigade's collapse ten days later. HBR holds a similar view on this.

> (d) Our not supporting SINGJANG brought home to the Chinese our weaknesses as also our poor leadership responsible for bringing about such a situation.
>
> 53. Thus the battle of SINGJANG could well perhaps be the point where the die was cast for the pattern of fighting that subsequently took place in the KAMENG Frontier Division.

Then after the valiant resistance of Maj Chaudhury's men all morning, the inevitable happened. When the situation got impossible, he was ordered to withdraw at 1230 hrs. The men crossed over via Bridge V and reported back by 1536.

Military historian, Major General PJS Sandhu (retired) claims fR71 that the PLA let off the surviving Indians and al- lowed them to carry their 11 wounded (6 were killed and 5 more reported missing. However, HBR mentions 7 dead and 7 missing. Peking radio reported 100 Chinese casualties) and return to the Army's lines while the Chinese themselves properly cremated the 6 dead Punjabis. This is supported by the HBR.

(c) The Chinese allowing our troops to withdraw, which the former could have prevented, may well have had its subtle effect later.

Was this a token of goodwill and a conciliatory message (in keeping with the "safety valve" built into the 22-point charter given by General Luo Ruiqing (chief of staff of China's Central Military Commission), to PLA forces in the western sector (Ladakh) - "Only if Indian forces advanced to within 50 meters of PLA positions and Chinese forces could not survive without self-defence, would PLA forces prepare for self-defence. If the enemy then withdrew, PLA forces would not seek to block that withdrawal)" - or was it to cam- ouflage the Chinese plans for the all-out, no-quarters-given attack to come soon?

Operation Leghorn- the layout, deployment and movement of Indian forces, on the morning of 10 October.

October 10th afternoon to the night of 19th - those fateful ten days of command paralysis: Geo-strategic, operational and tactical.

Kaul's request for a personal visit to Delhi was granted. He left Namka chu on 10th and arrived at Delhi on October 11.

[**Note:** Before leaving, he ordered the *GOC* of 4 Division, Parshad, that all offensive plans were to be held in abeyance and the present line was to be defended. This order is to be noted and we will bring this up in our analysis, soon. Also, Kaul took his time, casually, and confirmed the above verbal order in writing on October 13, late in the day. For inexplicable reasons (other than a casual approach?) he did this after returning to his HQ at Tezpur, having spent two days with the Army top brass in Delhi, though the decision for holding the status quo, was endorsed at the highest levels, in the late evening of October 11.

The order read:

- The bridges along Namka-chu from Bridge I (MM9114) to temporary log bridges (MM8317) **will** be held (in the south) at all costs.

- Line of communications via Lumpu (MM8906)

will be protected.

- Hathung-la-MM8913 (south of Namka-chu) will be held.

- Tsangley-MM7719, **will** be held at the *discretion of* GOC, *4 Division.*

It is contextual to this article, to point out that in the October 11 meeting at Delhi, where Kaul presented the grim reality at Namka-chu, Nehru asked Thapar and Sen for their views, they both agreed with the proposal to call of any of- fensive action and hold the present positions, but they didn't favour any relocation of the Army's defences to more convenient sites.

Please note that none of these officers had been physically anywhere near the theatre of action. Kaul's belated visit to the Namka-chu valley offered the *only* first-hand peek at what the situation on the ground was. We don't know whether the observations and analyses of the only officer who had studied and reported on the military-tactical possibilities of this theatre, Captain Mahavir Prasad of 1 Sikh, had been conveyed to these exalted quarters. But the bottom line is no relocation to better positions was sanctioned by IA's top brass that day.

Nehru then said, "If the odds were against us and if the commander on the spot so felt, then instead of attacking the Chinese, we should hold on to our present positions." *[Emphasis ours.}*

This runs contrary to the narrative of the political leadership imposing a suicidal course of action on the military, without reference to operational and tactical realities. It is clear that the Army's military commanders at the highest levels didn't want the 7 Brigade to be withdrawn from the exposed positions at Namka-chu for redeployment at a tactically and logistically more defensible location.

[Note: This was on October 11 - five days prior to the PLA S internal report on Indian intentions at Namka-chu was submitted by General Lei Ying Fu to Mao and five days before Mao decided to destroy Indian forces in the Namka- chu area through an all-out offensive.]

This should be read along with Menon's instructions after his September 22 meeting with Thapar, which read:

"... the chief of Army staff was accordingly directed to take action for the eviction of the Chinese from the Kameng Frontier Division in Nefa **as soon as he is ready."** *[Emphasis ours.}*

No date or deadline was set for this action.

> 28. The Chief of the Army Staff then asked for written instructions of the Government to evict the Chinese in DHOLA area. The following Government directions were then given:-
>
> > "The decision throughout has been as discussed at previous meetings that the Army should prepare and throw the Chinese out as soon as possible. The Chief of the Army Staff was accordingly directed to take action for the eviction of the Chinese in KAMENG Frontier Division of NEFA as soon as he is ready."
>
> 29. Army Headquarters, in turn, issued these directions on 22 September 1962 to both Western and Eastern Commands. (Annexure 25).

HBR

Therefore, the original political decision to evict the Chinese from Indian territory was made contingent upon military preparations and operational/tactical convenience as considered appropriate by Thapar. And it was Thapar who must bear the cross for the timing and operationalization of this order. More so since he, along with Sen and Kaul, knew that they had not made any provisions for creation of the logistic and operational bases in support of the forward staging areas, as had been originally instructed by the govt.

Is there a mitigating factor here for these three officers? Documents do show that AHQ had requested the government for resources to help ramp up the formations as per requirement. The government had not responded helpfully. Therefore, doesn't that make the Forward Policy non-operational in essence? Did these officers and gentlemen stand their ground on this vital aspect?

When we read the Indian narratives, we get overwhelmed by the plethora of problems cited. But do we ask the basic tactical questions? We are told that the 7 Brigade was ham- strung by the insane order to attack Thag-la and its units were therefore strung out in untenable positions.

However, we have seen earlier here that Kaul had can- celled that order before he left the area on October 11 morn- ing. He had ordered a defensive deployment. The same re- vised order was confirmed at the highest levels of the govern- ment and the army by the night of October 11.

So, in the intervening 10 days before the Chinese attack on the October 20, Dalvi was free to organise his defences. Or are we missing something here?

The missing links are provided by the **HBR** as under:

> 6. The NAMKA CHU River line continued to be held from Bridge 1 to Bridge 5, a distance of some 10 miles, on the orders of the Corps Commander, after the SINGJANG Battle on 10 October and later confirmed by signal on 13 October Annexure 95). Orders for reinforcement of TSANGLE were given by the Corps Commander as late as 18 October and reiterated on 19 October (Annexures 102 and 103). We have seen the advice given by the Brigadier General Staff to the Corps Commander for thinning out from the NAMKA CHU Area and withdrawing from TSANGLE (Appendix D, Para 30). We have also seen the repeated representations by the Divisional Commander to the Corps Commander for a decision to organise our positions along the NAMKA CHU and the evacuation of TSANGLE. All these had but little success. (Annexure 94).
>
> 7. The net result, however, was that the River line was held and TSANGLE NOT only held but reinforced. In the meantime, the River had appreciably gone down and, by 19/20 October, was easily fordable. (Report of Commanding Officer 9 PUNJAB, Paras 16 and 17 - Annexure 146). Thus the holding of the Bridges had little meaning.

9. The Brigade Commander, therefore, on 19 October, strongly represented to the Divisional Commander the seriousness of the situation. He pointed out over the telephone that, with the over-stretched defence layout of the Brigade, the enemy had the capacity to drive a wedge and strike at TSANGDHAR. The Brigade Commander, therefore,

TOP SECRET

TOP SECRET

180

wanted urgent permission to withdraw all troops located WEST of Bridge 4. This would have released him an equivalent of a battalion strength to re-deploy on a reduced frontage and, thus, make the defences more compact and stronger.

10. The Brigade Commander's feelings on the subject can be gauged from his concluding remarks to the Divisional Commander. These were "I am NOT prepared to stand by and watch my troops massacred. It is time someone took a firm stand. If the higher authorities wanted a scapegoat, I am prepared to offer myself and put in my papers on this issue". (The Brigade Major's Report - Annexure 147 - and Statement of Commander 4 Artillery Brigade - Annexure 148, Para 21). A message incorporating the text of the conversation was also passed on to the Division.

11. The Brigade Commander had represented almost daily before this, but, by 19 October, he had reached the end of his tether. It is apparent so had the Chinese. They struck the next morning.

So, does it seem that Kaul and the AHQ had "hardened" their stance after their October 11 meltdown? The matter gets murky as well as quirky at this point.

Kaul had himself seen what was going on and particularly the state of supplies and logistics. He saw that basic covering fire to the 9 Punjab - contingent, couldn't be provided, when they were bravely battling it out at Tseng Jong. Nehru had given a free hand to Thapar and Sen. What changed after that

> 73. In the meantime, the Brigadier General Staff IV Corps had made an appreciation on the DHOLA situation. This also clearly brought out that TSANGLE should be evacuated and the DHOLA garrison thinned out. (Appendix D to 4 Division letter No 302/10/GS(OPS) of 16 October 1962 - Annexure 94 - Report of Brigadier General Staff IV Corps (Appendix D) - Statement of Chief Engineer IV Corps (Annexure 84)).
>
> 74. In spite of all this advice, the Corps Commander insisted that all Brigades will be held and there will be NO thinning out from DHOLA Area. Indeed, he went a step further and, on 14 October, he countermanded his orders of 10 October regarding TSANGLE. On 10 October, the discretion for holding TSANGLE was given to the Divisional Commander. On 14 October, he ordered that TSANGLE will be held at all cost (Annexure 95).
>
> 75. The reasons for Corps Commander insisting on keeping the ill-fated Brigade in their tactically unsound positions and holding on to TSANGLE at all costs cannot be fathomed. Perhaps, there were pressures from DELHI. In this connection it must be brought out that TEZPUR was specially linked to DELHI by a direct trunk route.
>
> 76. The behind-the-scene collusion between the Corps Commander and the General Staff at Army Headquarters is well brought out by implication/the developments on 16 October. On that day the Corps Commander presumably discussed the situation either with the Officiating Chief of the General Staff or the Director of Military Operations. The subsequent signals that must have been arranged between them crossed each other and were not with the recipients when they sent their own. The coincidence regarding action in TSANGLE in the two signals is worthy of note.

HBR

Did the apparent sanity that had returned on October 11 had evaporated in three days? Let's see what indicators can be found in the **HBR** analyses here:

(a) neither the Chief of the Army Staff nor the Army Commander knew the exact strength at TSANGLE, and hence, Chief of the Army Staff could not possibly be a party to have ordered a battalion to TSANGLE. Presumably, Lt Gen KAUL and the General Staff required on paper Chief of the Army Staff's authority for the reinforcing of TSANGLE.

(b) the initiative of continuing to hold TSANGLE and, if possible, reinforce it, was that of the Corps Commander. In this he was perhaps abetted by the General Staff at Army Headquarters, but Chief of the Army Staff was not in the picture.

(c) Chief of the Army Staff and the Army Commander were clearly reconciled to the idea that operations were to be postponed to April/May 1963.

(d) the General Staff Branch Army Headquarters and the Corps Commander had NOT yet given up the idea of immediate operations. General Staff Branch Army Headquarters did not indicate the planning date for operations as April/May 1963 in their signal.

81. It is significant that the Corps Commander in his signal did not ask or suggest that the Brigade should be redeployed despite all the advice he got from his staff and 4 Divisional Commander.

(IV Corps Signal No 03116 of 16 October, 1962 - Annexure 96)
(Eastern Command Signal No 02278 of 16 October- Annexure 97)
(Army Headquarters Signal No 161354/MO1 of
(16 October 1962 - Annexure 98.

95. The defences in the DHOLA Area were the concern of the Corps Commander and, as such, he should have ordered the redeployment of the Brigade, when he realised the strength and superiority of the enemy. It was on his express orders that

TOP SECRET

TOP SECRET

103

the positions along the River NAMKA CHU were continued to be held by 7 Infantry Brigade.

> 101   Finally, the continued occupation of TSANGLE and the keeping of 7 Infantry Brigade in unsound tactical positions against all military advice was entirely the responsibility of the Corps Commander. In this he was probably abetted by the Officiating Chief of the General Staff and the Director of Military Operations.

Here, it seems that the earlier intransigence of Thapar and Sen during Kaul's briefing in Delhi, had been replaced by pragmatism in the next few days, while Kaul had relapsed into his "Wild West" ways?

But then, Kaul has gone on record saying that this was not his own stance, but his superiors prevailed upon him, against his express advice to the contrary. Take a look:

> 82   On 17 October, the Defence Minister, Chief of the Army Staff, and the Army Commander visited TEZPUR. Lt Gen KAUL in his report (Appendix B, paragraph 18) states that these three reiterated the necessity of holding on to TSANGLE and our positions along the NAMKA CHU against his advice.
>
> 83   The holding of the NAMKA CHU has already been discussed and there seems to be no reason why Chief of the Army Staff or the Army Commander should have taken up such strong views on the dispositions of the Brigade. This especially when their knowledge of the detailed dispositions was from the Corps Commander himself. Regarding TSANGLE, the signal (0213D of 17 October 1962 - Annexure 99) sent by the Corps Commander to 4 Infantry Division on 17 October is revealing. The operative paragraph on TSANGLE reads:-
>
>> "After considering various factors involved Government have directed that TSANGLE will continue to be held with the present strength at my discretion".

HBR

So, was Kaul lying - on record? Someone was lying here for sure. Was Krishna Menon whispering in his protege's ears even at this late date when the crisis was reaching a crescendo? We have seen earlier here that Menon had for- bidden the keeping of records and minutes of his meetings. But then what kept Thapar and Sen from stepping in?

Though the Henderson Brooks Report seems to surmise that all the blame lay at the door of Kaul, do the documented facts revealed this far, absolve the other two officers? During the meeting with Nehru on the evening of October 11, did not the chief of the Army staff, Thapar, and GOC-in-C Eastern Army, Sen, shoot down Kaul's proposal to relocate the brigade?

We don't really see any evidence here to believe that these two officers were not party to this painful command failure at the operational level. So let us take a look at the rel- evant part of the published memoirs of a key figure in the dramatis personae, who had a direct role in this affair. And in the process let us re-examine the other oft repeated theme of political (and civilian) interference in military decision-mak- ing. Bhola Nath Mullik, was heading the Intelligence Bureau

of India since 1950 and was deeply involved in all aspects of the strategy to face Chinese intrusions across Indian borders.

He is on record *IRBI,* describing a meeting at Tezpur, IV Corps HQ, on the morning of 17th October, where the final decision to stay put at Namka Chu was taken.

He says:

- Kaul and his corps staff were adamant that 7 Brigade will not be able to hold the Namka chu posi- tions since the Chinese were vastly superior in eveiy respect. Hence, they recommended withdrawal to more suitable locations.
- Inspector General, Assam Rifles recommended the same for all his forces in the newly created posts.
- COAS, Gen Thapar and GOC Eastern Command, Lt Gen Sen, both, insisted on holding Tsangle and the Namka chu line.
- Krishna Menon, the defence minister, vehemently argued against any withdrawals since that would give away land to the Chinese and change the status quo on the McMahon Line. He was concerned about Indian public

opinion, in case of territorial losses to China.

- At Mullik's suggestion, the three Generals (Thapar, Sen and Kaul) had a closed-door meeting for two hours without any civilian presence or interference.

- *When the three emerged from the meeting, the decision was* announced that the earlier stance of Generals Thapar and Sen holds good and status quo is to be maintained in this area. Certain other related de- cisions were also announced about stepping up sup- plies and reinforcements.

Readers will find it easy now, to come to their own con- clusions on the vexed question of culpability for the fatal rigidity at the Namka chu front.

But does this automatically translate into the disaster that befell 7 Brigade three days later? In our off-the-record discuss-ions with military commanders at the highest levels, we have tried to understand what could have possibly deterred Parshad and Dalvi from reorienting their defences at the Namka-chu theatre in the time they had, after Kaul's order to go on the defensive.

"Holding the bridges" on Namka-chu can be interpreted as denying their usage by the enemy. The river by now was a shallow stream, with the water level having come down sub- stantially. Now the bridges were anyway not obstacles to the PLA crossing over anymore. India had artillery and heavy mortars on Tsangdhar. MMGs would be covering the bridges and the other side of the river. Why was it essential to hold on to that "T-shaped" deployment with no depth and no re- serves, for interception and counter attacks?

How could the Chinese 155 and 157 regiments infiltrate so easily and successfully? They infiltrated in strength, pene- trated to the rear, and got in among the Indian positions. And they didn't just take the Rajputs by surprise. E troop, 17 Para FR's gun positions on the Tsangdhar ridge were virtually un- defended, inspite of its criticality for the entire brigade de- fences. 2nd Lieutenant Behl found no infantry support avail- able, no sign of the two 1/9 GR platoons deployed on the ridge, anywhere near his guns!

Commanding heights of Thag-la or shortage of supplies have nothing to do with this monumental blunder in de- fence. And no, higher commands didn't not hand down this defensive plan per se. It is true that the local command had been denied the prerogative of "thinning down" the defences by the river. But did that construe the dictating of actual field deployment of units and companies?

> 63. The question where the Brigade should take up its defences was a tactical problem and at best could only be decided by the Field Formation Commanders concerned. The most that could be laid down at Government and Army Headquarters level was perhaps that NO territory SOUTH of the NAMKA CHU River should be lost. The question of how much and where to hold was certainly not possible at that level. Even if this was suggested, it is considered that the Corps Commander, especially Lt Gen BM KAUL, had sufficient standing and influence to position the Brigade, as he thought best.

HBR

As we can see, Kaul had himself "made the bed on which he lay" in his brief sojourn at Namka-chu. Now, on the eve of the day of reckoning, while he lay ill on a hospital bed far away, 7 Brigade lay strewn out along a distant river valley, sans any tactical considerations, let down by senior officers who the juniors trusted upon to do the right thing, waiting for a fate its men didn't deserve.

```
66.     The Brigade continued to be deployed, non-tactically
along the NAMKA CHU guarding the bridges. The detailed
deployment on 19 October 1962 is given below:-

        (a) Brigade Headquarters            DHOLA

        (b) 4 GRENADIERS less one
            company                          Bridge 1

            One company                      KHINZAMANE Area

                        TOP SECRET
```

```
                        TOP SECRET
                             66
        (c) 9 PUNJAB less one company        Bridge 2

            One company                      TSANGLE

        (d) 1/9 GORKHA RIFLES less one
            company and one platoon          As Brigade reserve
                                             near Brigade
                                             Headquarters.

            One company                      Moving to TSANGLE

            One platoon                      TSANGDHAR

        (e) 2 RAJPUT                         Bridge 3, 4, and
                                             Log Bridge.
```

HBR

Here a parallel can be drawn with what happened a decade later regarding India Gandhi's directions to Manekshaw about military operations in East Pakistan in 1971. In both instances the government of the day left it to the military to decide upon the timing and operational parameters of execution of political mandates. In the case of Namka- chu, this political mandate was revised within three weeks (on October 11, after Kaul's briefing) upon advice of the military.

The new mandate of calling off the attack and holding the positions, didn't go far enough to address the realities on ountability for this debacle lie only at the top? To understand this in all its nuances, let us examine the tortuous path that led he Indian army to the Namka chu valley in the first place.

Who and what led the Indian army into the Namka chu trap?

Operation Leghorn on October 10th was a failure. And the subsequent ten days leading to the disaster on the 20th, were wasted through inaction. But what led to this mess in the first place? How did the Indian army find itself in this predicament to begin with?

Now, let us look at the operationalisation of the Forward Policy in the Tawang sector earlier that year and the curious matter of the Army's appropriation of and interference in political decisions, at lower levels, nearer to the ground. This makes for interesting reading, in the context of the narrative on "political interference" in military matters and the "irresponsible" Forward Policy being pushed by the government.

Parshad is supposed to have mentioned to Kaul, during his visit in the forward areas that in early August, he had recommended the occupation of the tactically dominant Thag-la ridge (grid ref: 8717), *which was our territory and free of the Chinese then.*

Major General Niranjan Parshad (image source unknown).

A little background here would be in order. In June 1961, the Chinese seriously encroached upon India territory and patrolled inside Indian areas between three and four miles west of the Khinzemane Post (grid ref: MM9415) and adjoining grazing grounds, which India claimed. This post is a landmark because the Khinzemane route was taken by the Dalai Lama, ill and weak with dysentery, when escaping from the Chinese in Tibet, in 1959.

That was the point till which his Tibetan National Volunteer Defence Army escorts and the two CIA radio operators had accompanied him when he crossed over on March31-April 1. This post remained disputed and a reference point for disputes and negotiations.

According to SIB (Subsidiary Intelligence Bureau) officer LD Kumar, India's old border post at Khinzemane was 1.5 miles (2.4 kilometres) to the south of the new post and the Chinese officials had been persuaded by SIB people, with great difficulty to accept the location of the new post, by "pulling a fast one" about "maps" which they had "forgotten to bring" (this was an excuse cooked up by Kumar to fend off the Chinese official for the moment!).

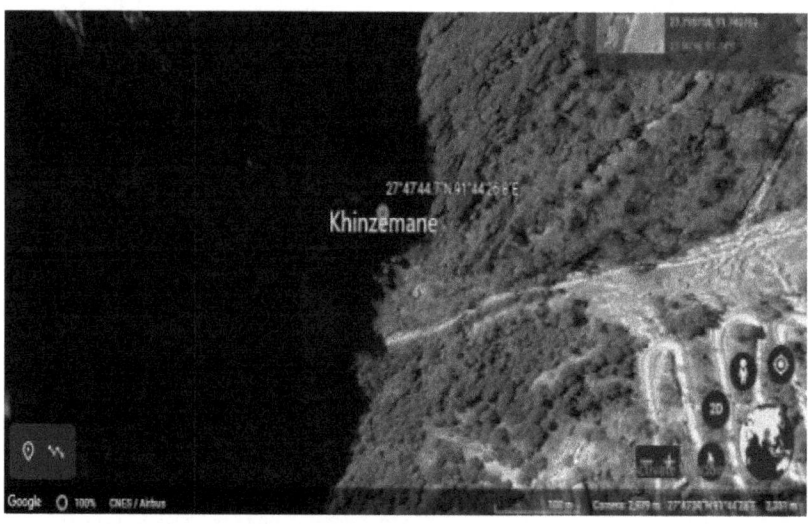

A closer look at the Khinzemane grazing grounds

Like any sovereign nation that takes its borders seriously, Sen had asked the AHQ for permission to patrol this particular stretch of Indian territory, west of Khinzemane, near the McMahon Line, in the coming patrolling season. Accordingly, AHQ issued instructions on April 27 that patrolling could be done west of Khinzemane, up to the McMahon Line and posts could be set up near the trijunction of India-Bhutan-Tibet (grid ref: MM7914) without prior sanction. [Emphasis ours.}

The task given to Eastern Command by AHQ in April 62: India - Bhutan- Tibet trijunction shown to the left, ultimately the new post was located at The Dong pastures (Dhola post), existing Kkinzemane post on the right

It is while studying the execution of this AHQ order, that we find a series of interesting revelations, which hold the key to the subsequent debacle at Narnka-chu.

"The McMahon Line - Here we come!"

Let us start with the politics around it. Since the Indo- China border dispute is historically linked to "differing perceptions" [R9], it is important to note that in the Nefa, the McMahon Line is a clearly drawn boundary, whose wisdom and methodology may be disputed on technical grounds, but not its location on the map. The Shimla Convention of 1914, between British India, the Tibetan government, and its sovereign overlord - the Republic of China, produced this boundary with clearly laid down coordinates.

Subsequently the Chinese government disputed that part of the agreement which dealt with the demarcation of the areas under the Tibetan government's authority (the Blue Line) and those directly under Chinese administration (hence Ivan Chen, the Chinese representative didn't sign the final agreement). However, the part demarcating the India-Tibet border (the Red Line, which is commonly known as the McMahon Line) over 890 kilometres from the north eastern extremity of Bhutan to the Isu-Razi pass on the Burma (now Myanmar) border, remained undisputed between the respective signatories - Henry McMahon, foreign secretary of British India And Lonchen Satrafrom the Tibetan side.

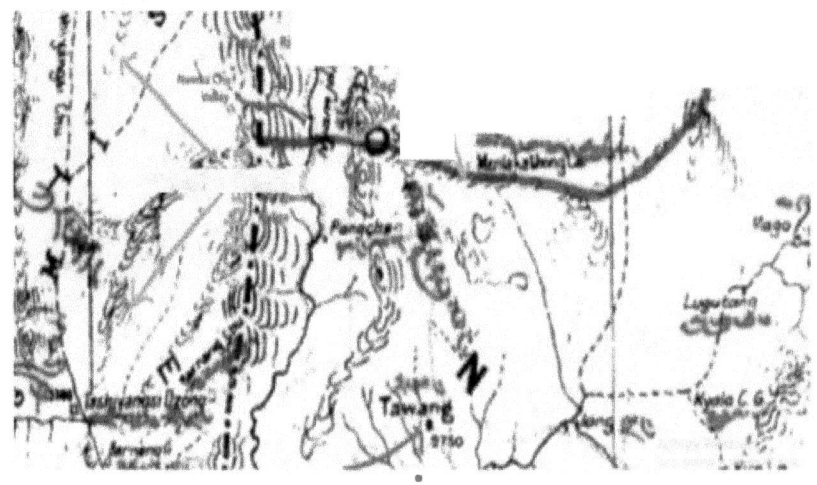

McMahon Line as plotted in the Simla Convention with our markings ofre/,event features.

Legally, the McMahon line is ironclad from the perspective of international law. However, both China and India kept disputing it on technicalities and then again quoting it, as per their convenience. India argued that the "spirit" of the Shimla Convention's "inner line" - border between Tibet - and India as against the "outer line" - border between area controlled by Tibetan government and what came under direct Chinese administration - was based on the natural "watershed" features.

This passes over the Thag-la ridge, north of the Namka- chu valley and, hence, includes the Khinzemane grazing grounds, in the Niyamjang-chu valley (see the images above). Whereas the map signed off by the British and Tibetan representatives clearly shows the boundary starting from the tri-junction between Bhutan, Tibet and India (as shown in the images above) and running across the Tsangdhar ridge, due east, for quite a bit.

The ambiguities which may have appeared to be of no critical consequence once upon a time, provided the flash point once both sides started "pushing" and jostling all along the frontier. We will come back to revisit this vexed issue of the alignment of this line as the story progresses.

THE HIDDEN KEY TO NAMKA CHU MYSTERY OF CAPTAIN MAHAVIR PRASAD'S PATROL, HIS REPORT IGNORED & A HISTORICAL INJUSTICE DONE TO HIM; MAO CHOOSES WAR - THE CASUS BELLI; INDIAN ARMY WOBBLES - 'NEITHER CAUTIOUS LEGALITY NOR PRE-EMPTIVE BOLDNESS

The mystery of Captain Mahavir Prasad's patrol, its tragic aftermath and the historic injustice done to him.

When discussing the Namka-chu battle, *all* historical and military accounts talk about one Captain Mahavir Prasad, Maha Vir Chakra, of 1 Sikh, who took a patrol to the Namka-chu area and set up the Dho-la post. Most analysts and narratives imply that Prasad erred in setting up the post at that lo- cation. The story goes that he gave precedence to issues of logistics and convenience in selecting the location rather than tactical considerations. All accounts agree that the Thag- la ridge, atop the slopes to the north of Namka-chu valley, was the best site for a post militarily[R10].

History, until now, has blanked out the story of Prasad beyond this point in the narrative and mentions him as a footnote later when he fell in battle, on the morning of October 20.

On May 15, 1962, Prasad took a patrol consisting of the No. 4 platoon of 5 Assam Rifles, three intelligence men from the SIB (one officer plus two constables), a sepoy from 1 Sikh and 150 porters from Lumpu (grid ref: MM8906) towards the Namka-chu area. After two days of trekking with the full team, on May 17, Prasad took the SIB officer, LD Kumar for a reconnaissance mission, ahead of the team, to locate a suitable location for the post, which had been ordered to be setup according to the AHQ's order quoted above.

The two of them climbed up to the Tsangdhar ridge (MM8115) on the south side of the Namka-chu (river). According to the briefing received by Prasad, this was the area where the post was to be set up.

[*Note: This will come up for analysis and we will discuss the responsibility and accountability.*]

Prasad finally chose Tse-dong, (which he reported to be at grid ref: MM 8416) a small pasture, at 11,500-12,000 feet, on the slopes above Namka-chu, leading up to the Tsangdhar ridge, as the most suitable site for the post. This later came to be known as the "Dho-la post" and has been a subject of in- tense debate and scrutiny over the last 60 years.

Dho-la post at Tse-dong pasture as seen from the north west. Tsangdhar ridge is to the right (south), Thagla ridge is to the left (north), across Namka chu

Subsequently, as we shall see, XXXIII Corps quoted MM8316 as the actual grid reference for the post, whereas Prasad had used this reference (MM8316) for a hut 300 feet above the Dho-la post, which he had recommended as an OP (observation post). To confuse things further, in the report sent to the corps from the 4 Division, (presumably) the reference for the Dho-la post, was apparently given as MM8513 -

as later mentioned by the corps to the Eastern Army and AHQ (this correspondence from XXXIII Corps, of August 1962, has been quoted later in this article).

Captain Mahavir Prasad (From Maj General Krishen Khorana's personal collections).

The word on the street is that Prasad was not even debriefed when he returned after the long, 45-day patrol, although quoting him and mentioning his patrol are de rigueur in any story about Namka-chu. More on this military hypocrisy later.

Thus confusion, misrepresentation, and a cavalier approach to critical matters, ran like a common thread through this entire Namka-chu-Dho-la post saga.

On May 18 and 19, Prasad continued with his patrolling of other features in the area. He climbed up the slopes to the north of Namka-chu and checked out Thag-la (MM8717), the much-talked-about tactical "magic feature", which we didn't occupy and, hence, the myth goes that we lost the battle at Namka-chu. The route to Thag-la from Tse-dong (Dho-la post) was via a nine-mile-long track, crossing the Namka-chu (river), over the log bridge at MM8318. Then the track climbed steeply up the northern slope for 1,000 feet and

turned east, following an easier gradient all the way up to Thag-la (pass). The one-way straight trek would take fit troops, travelling with normal packs, three hours. He returned to Tse-dong after patrolling the prominent features on the other side to evaluate the best location for the post.

Captain Mahavir Prasad's patrolling zone

Upon his return to Tse-dong, and the gradual arrival of his team with building material and store stocks, work started on setting up the post, and was completed by June 4. Prasad continued to patrol other features all around the area, on both sides of Namka-chu between the India-Bhutan-Tibet trijunction.

*[**Note:** The original map coordinates are- MM7915 but claimed by Prasad to be at MM7522 and Khinzemane post to*

the east at MM9415].

Here comes the crux of the issue.

Why was Thag-la not occupied? Why was the Dho-la post located at Tse-dong? What were the considerations? On whose orders was the post continued at that location (in spite of later claims from the Army's top brass that it was neither legally unambiguous nor tactically suitable)? What were the operational and tactical implications militarily? And most importantly, what were the political implications?

> 35   DHOLA Post was established NORTH of the McMAHON Line as shown on maps prior to October/November 1962 edition. It is believed the old edition was given to the Chinese by our External Affairs Ministry to indicate the McMAHON Line. It is also learnt that we tried to clarify the error in our maps, but the Chinese did not accept our contention. The General Staff must have been well aware of this; and it was their duty to have warned lower formations regarding the dispute. This was not done, and the seriousness of the establishment of the DHOLA Post was not fully known to lower formations.

HBR

So, who has the right decide and act on these "ambiguities"? Is it for a nation's military, at the subsector level (Kameng Frontier Division), to take it upon themselves, to change maps and boundaries? Who was authorized to sanction the infringement of the McMahon Line in the western subsector (Kameng) in Nefa?

Let us look at the political consequences of playing around with the McMahon Line in the Kameng Frontier Division.

Mao's distrust and resentment towards Nehru, as we have repeatedly mentioned here, was deep-seated and intractable on grounds of "class" and ideology. His long-term plan to settle scores with Nehru's India for its involvement with, and support to, the Tibetan rebels, was held in abeyance under situational constraints in 1959.

Those constraints emanated from the state of China's domestic economy as well as international pressures. The US, the Soviet Union and the fraternal enemy, Taiwan, were all hostile to Mao's China in their own ways.

However, Mao was a chess player. He was waiting for India to push things beyond the threshold and bring it upon themselves. And that's what India did, as per Mao's paradigm, by staking claim, through military presence, to territories beyond the official McMahon Line, in the Namka-chu area [RII]

This layout, as seen from Tibet, the origi,nal Mc Mahon Line is shown, passing over Tsangdhar while Indias claim line passes over Thag-la

It is to be noted that though China disputed the McMahon Line officially as the legitimate border, it was willing to live with it as an arrangement that allows conflicting parties to coexist peacefully, until a final settlement is reached. However, when the Army's local military commanders crossed that disputed McMahon Line too and tried to reinterpret it on the ground, it was the proverbial last straw for Mao.

This led to a chain of events, leading to a pitched battle on 10 October which provided the casus belli for China's military offensive on 20 October 1962.

In June 1962, China's ambassador to Poland, Wang Bingnan, was assured by the US Ambassador, Jacob D Beam, that

America, under the present circumstances, would not support a Taiwanese attack on mainland China. In the mean- time, the crisis in Laos too was capped by the big powers. And just as the situation at Namka-chu escalated through September and October, the Cuban missile crisis too was as- suming dangerous dimensions.

The Soviet Union, on the backfoot on the Cuban crisis, needed solidarity within the "Communist Block". Thus, there was no question of President Krushchev's acting against China's interests at that moment.

For the first time in years, China saw a window of opportunity in the east (Indian borders) where it could go for limited aggression without fear of a larger conflagration.

In the meantime, India had ample evidence of China's sensitivity over Thag-la. The SIB team accompanying Prasad on one of his patrols to Thag-la, in May 1962, found a wooden board with a specific warning that this was Chinese territory. This coupled with the SIB team leader Kumar's earlier experience with his Chinese counterpart over the Khinzemane post, which was a matter for serious consideration. But such political nuances were missed by the Army's local commands with disastrous consequences.

> 31. An incident of some interest to the above recommendations had occurred in the meantime and requires note. A Subsidiary Intelligence Bureau representative, on a reconnaissance of the area of THAGLA Ridge had found a wooden plank on 23 May 1962 with Chinese characters. These were later translated at TEZPUR and read "This is our river and mountain". This was conveyed by 4 Infantry Division to XXXIII Corps, Eastern Command, and Army Headquarters on 12 July 1962. (Annexure 43). This then was another pointer that NAMKA CHU and the THAGLA Ridge were sensitive areas.

HBR

[Note: Here we must point out for those in today's India, talking casually about Indian border territories in Ladakh and Arunachal as "disputed areas'; this is what the Chinese "perception" of those disputed areas are]

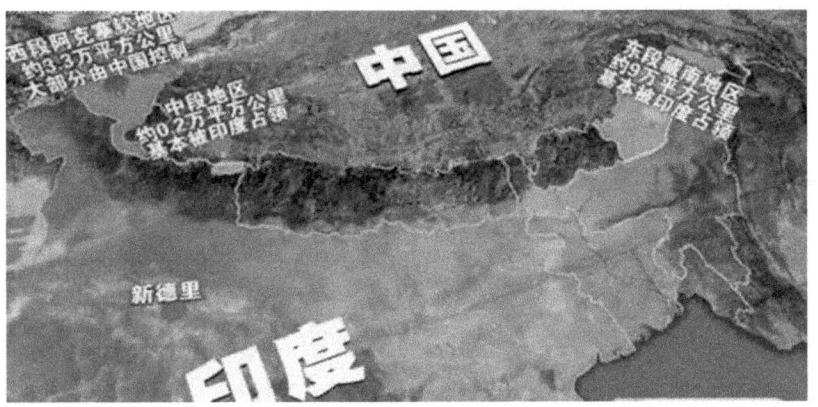

China claims portion marked in orange in Ladakh and marked green in Arunachal Pradesh.

Now, let us come to the military and tactical considera- tions. Prasad's assessment of the ground, from the perspec- tive of a CDL (company-defended locality) was as discussed below:

The McMahon Line in the Namka-chu area and the approaches to Tawang (via Lumpu), in case of a Chinese attack, would be best defended by a platoon post at Tsangle, one at Hathung-la, with Company HQ plus 1 platoon at either Tsedong (Dho-la post) or Thag-la. These posts would be mutually supporting, located at tactical hubs, and covering all the axes towards Lumpu (and further onto Zemithang-Shakti-Tawang).

His opinion was that the Dho-la post had the advantage of covering all the tracks from Namka-chu up the southern slopes; It was not easy to "creep up" on; It had an excellentview of the Thag-la (pass) which would be definitely used by the Chinese. It was much more easily maintainable than other comparable locations.

He found both Tsangdhar and Thag-la ridges to be cov- ered in deep snow for many months and hence unsuitable for stable posts. Thagla was also a much longer and difficult haul for porters, from Indian supply bases.

In case of full-blown war, Prasad was categorical that Tse Dong (Dho-la post) would be "suicidal" to fight in. It would be cut off and destroyed, he said, as it happened in the actual event. But then, in his opinion, **Thagla was *also* untenable as an FDL for more than 3 days.** His thorough patrolling revealed that Thagla would be easily cut off by enemy forces infiltrating through Karpo-la II and Namdang-la (MM7822).

Have we ever heard of this last bit from any "authoritative" source or found any mention of this crucial fact in any standard narrative? As we shall see in this story, holding Thag-la became an idee fixe for the 4 Division, XXXIII Corps and subsequently both the Eastern Army and the AHQ. They made the primacy of Thag-la (and hence its occupation) a key proposition in their operational plans for this area. Through the decades, since the tragedy of Namka-chu, a bi- nary proposition has been an essential part of the narrative: "Thag-la or nothing! Thag-la good, Dho-la bad (so very Orwellian!)".

No one seems to have taken on board the fact that Captain Prasad was the ONLY Indian army officer to have ever visited the Tsangdhar - Dho-la post area before 9 Punjab arrived in the latter half of September '62. He was also the ONLY Indian army officer to have ever visited the Thag-la ridge and pass, till Major M.S. Chaudhary went up to Tseng Jong, en route to Thagla, with his 50 man-force in October. Yet, NO ONE paid heed to his first-hand observations on the reality of Thag -la as a battle post.

(Brigadier Indrajeet (Injo) Gakhal (Retd.), who served later with Capt. Prasad's unit, 1 Sikh, shared with this author, on

a recorded video session, his strong views on this matter. The Namka chu river lay between the two ridges Tsangdhar to the south, on whose slopes lay Tseng Jong (Dho-la post) and Thag-la to the north, on the crest of which lay the Thag-la pass. He was certain that as an infantry officer, he would have preferred to have a river obstacle in front, rather than behind him, astride a tenuous line of communications & support [R12].

However, it is to be noted that Prasad conceptualized a 7company-level operation at Namka-chu, on the Indian side. His entire assessment and prognosis were based on that scale. As it turned out within three months of his return from that area, it became the scene of a much larger operation, involving a brigade for India and the equivalent of a division for China. Obviously, the deployment plan and tactical factors would be different. But the fundamentals of terrain, topography, ordnance, and logistics would remain the same. Of particular interest here is the fact that it had taken 150 porters (apparently that was the maximum number of locals who were available at any given point in time, for this purpose) accompanying Prasad, in May, to carry material and supplies for the Dho-la post housing one Assam Rifles platoon. One can imagine the manpower needed to transport supplies for a four battalion-brigade.

Thus, the decision to air drop supplies on the Tsangdhar ridge. And given the realities of the terrain and weather, the modest portion of those supplies actually reaching the Indian forces.

Now, let us have a look at how these abovementioned fac- tors played out in that area.

Both Tsangdhar and Thag-la ridges were difficult propositions for setting up a sustainable post. The slopes below Tsangdhar rolling down to the Namka-chu valley, had thick vegetation and foliage, with soggy ground underfoot. Thus 2- inch mortars would be ineffective against an incoming menace. They would burst against overhead foliage and their impact would be dulled by the soggy ground.

All areas from the top of Tsangdhar ridge downwards (not the Dho-la post alone) were within medium-machine gun (MMG) and heavy-mortar range from the opposite slopes (rising up to Thag-la) across Namka-chu. Thus, rein- forced bunkers and roofs were a must, wherever the post was put up. This factor cut both ways, so he recommended deployment of sufficient rifle grenades and grenade launchers in place of 2-inch mortars.

Even in those 24 days of Prasad's stay in that area, since the post was put up by June 4, four mortar-proof bunkers had already been constructed, out ofline of sight from Thag- la. Thus, in the 100-plus days after his leaving the post and the beginning of hostilities, how many more would have been constructed? According to him there was plenty of building material all around - solid timber.

[Note: By the way, the availability of food, from indige- nous plants and leaves and local game were plentiful for for- aging and hunting. This factor doesn't find mention in the official lore about the miserable supply situation at Namka- chu.]

Prasad had recommended a section post (observation post) to be set up 300 feet above Tse Dong's main platoon post. This was to obviate the possibility of being surprised by infiltration from across Namka-chu. His fall back plan for tenability of Indian positions in case of war, was to occupy Thag-la or Karpo-la I, although Thag-la too was not tenable beyond three days. **He** also advised regular patrolling from Dho-la post to cover the features on the opposite side, Thag- la, etc.

Therefore, how did the PLA pull a surprise by pushing a force across Thag-la, on September 8, 1962, and surrounded the Dho-la post? An enemy force just can't sneak up over and across the Thag-la feature, cross a 50 ft. wide waterbody (not generally fordable in September) in a such a manner. They had obviously been planning it for a while.

[Note: Here, the nearest PLA post, until then, was at Le, six miles from Khinzemane, in the Niyamjung-chu valley. Therefore, obviously there was a major military lapse on that score. Anyway, the option of moving base to Thag-la then obviously got knocked out after the PLA rolled down from its slopes.]

Thus, it transpires that Army's brigade and division commands didn't ensure patrolling of the Thag-la and other passes, in the days leading up to the Chinese deployment there, despite no permission being required from higher commands. Neither did they ensure the following of basic security protocol laid down by Prasad for early detection of Chinese incursion through the features across Namka-chu. Therefore, the implication parroted down the decades, blaming Prasad's setting up the post at Tse-dong, leaving Thag-la vacant doesn't hold water. Since all the other conditions he had put down as non-negotiable for the post's viabil-ity, were violated.

Political, strategic and operational considerations in the Tawang sector- whose decision was it anyway?

The plot further thickens as one goes deeper into the matter. In August 1962, after the Dho-la post had already been set up, the XXXIII Corps wrote to the Eastern Army a curious memo, arguing for the reinterpretation of the McMahon Line and urging for various serious actions, based on such military revision of the nation's political map. The memo went like this:

- The boundary line printed on the maps had considerable inaccuracies if the watershed principle and usage were to be applied.

- According to local inhabitants and political representatives who accompanied the Assam Rifles to the Oho-la Post, the accepted/recognized boundary was the one based on the watershed principle. Based on this, the proposal was to consider MM7522 as the new trijunction instead of MM79r4 as given in the of- ficial map. However, since no specific authority or document was quoted in the memo to establish this claim, it appears that local anecdotal hearsay became the basis of this bizarre proposal by the XXXIII Corps.

- To cover the three approach routes from Tibet into India from Khinzemane to the new trijunction, as per the watershed principle, it was proposed to set up two posts one, of course was on the Thag-la ridge (the Army's version of Shangrila, the tactical magic land for all seasons) and the other at Tsangle

(MM7719) which was in Bhutan. Thus, the XXXIII Corps arbitrarily recommended the infringement of two boundaries: the one with Tibet across the Tsangdhar ridge and the other with Bhutan.

[Note: For violating Bhutans sovereign territory, no "principle" or "usage" was quoted. And to top it all, Prasad's assessment that a post on the Thag-la ridge would not be tenable for more than three days, in case of war, was blanked out from the narrative by someone in the command hierarchy - at brigade, division or corps level.]

(a) The boundary line printed on the maps had considerable inaccuracies, if the watershed principle and usage were to be applied.

(b) According to local inhabitants (graziers) and the political representatives who accompanied the ASSAM Rifles to the DHOLA Post, the accepted/recognised boundary was the one based on the watershed principle. (The letter did not specify as to who accepted/recognised this boundary line). It was, however, common knowledge that the McMAHON Line was based on the watershed principle. The TRI-JUNCTION, according to the watershed principle, should be MM 7522 and not as shown in the map MM 7914.

(c) There were three important approaches on the watershed boundary that lead into our area between KHINZAMANE and the recommended TRI-JUNCTION MM 7522. The approaches were as under:-

   (i)   THAGLA MM 8717
   (ii) KARPOLA II MM 8321
   (iii) HAMDANGLA MM 7822

(d) XXXIII Corps recommended that one post should be established at THAGLA and another at TSANGLE MM 7719 to cover the other two passes. TSANGLE, as can be seen, according to the old boundary, was in BHUTAN. (BHUTAN incidentally did raise this question in October, when a representative of theirs approached Corps Headquarters).

(e) The letter went on to give recommendations for establishing these posts and also asked for a survey to be carried out. Pending approval of the recommendations, it was intended to carry out patrolling between KHINZAMANE and the Watershed TRI JUNCTION.

(f) The last paragraph of the letter is of some importance and is reproduced below:-

"It will be seen from Sketch P attached (Sketch H of this Review) that the DHOLA Post grid reference (MM 8513), as reported earlier, is not correct and should be MM 8316. However, to avoid alarm and queries from all concerned, it is proposed to continue using the present grid reference in the location statement and situation reports until such time the case is finally decided by you. We hope it meets with your approval."

This, in effect, meant that the post was actually NORTH of the McMAHON Line as then marked on the map. The location as given out MM 8513 was just SOUTH and MM 8316 just NORTH of the Line. (Though the sketch showed this, the letter was not clear, and it was never really expressly brought out till 12 September 1962.

HBR

- NOW comes the piece de resistance. In the last paragraph of the letter. XXXIII Corps writes:

- "It will be seen from sketch that the Dho-la post grid reference MM8513, as reported earlier, is not correct and should be MM8316. However, to avoid alarm and queries from all concerned, it is proposed to continue using the present grid reference in the location statement and situation reports [emphasis ours] until such time the case is decided by you."

- [Note: Although the fact of the Dho-la post being located beyond the McMahon Line was known clearly to the corps, the letter obfuscates the fact. It does not clearly mention such a major and critical transgression, in so many words. In fact, this important issue was never expressly brought up till the Chinese came and surrounded the post on 8 September. Readers should be made aware, in this context, that XXXIII Corps vide their letter of February 24, 1962, had specifically recommended the setting up of the post (west of Khinzemane) at the trijunction, southeast of Tsangle (grid ref: MM7914) where the McMahon Line starts as per the original map, depicting the Line going west, atop the Tsangdhar ridge.]

- The documents and conversations on record show, as above, that:

- Prasad, as patrol leader of 1 Sikh, first violated the McMahon Line in setting up the Dho-la post in June 1962. According to him, that was the area where he had been ordered to set up the post, as per his sand-model briefing.

- Parshad, GOC of 4 Division, responsible for the Kameng Frontier Division, was canvassing for further infringements of the McMahon Line, by moving even further north into the Thag La ridge

- Nathawat, GOC of XXXIII Corps, despite knowing about this infringement, condoned it and continued with the misrepresentation deliberately.

- Now, at this juncture, let us pause and ponder on these murky goings about a sensitive, and under the circumstances, explosive issue like the nation's borders.

- India steadfastly claimed the McMahon Line to be its legitimate border with Tibet, as inherited from the British Raj, legitimately, as per international law.

- The Chinese side was raising fundamental disputes on this "inheritance" both in the Nefa and Ladakh, calling it an unjust "colonial-imperial legacy". They were in fact claiming entire Nefa (90,000 square kilometres)

- Therefore, it was not in India's interest to discredit the McMahon Line in that volatile situation where China was looking for excuses to teach Nehru a les- son. That would be, aiding the Chinese design.

- These intricate political and legal matters are in the purview of the government and its specialized wings. Military officers at the unit and formation levels are neither qualified nor authorized to initiate material alterations to international boundaries through "fait accompli"actions.

- It was in the interest of the Chinese to dilute the legality and primacy of the McMahon Line through what aboutery and by ferreting out technical nuances.

- The local military commands' raising of the "watershed line" issue and precipitately acting on it with- out prior approval of the government was completely out of line. Therefore, it not just gift-wrapped an excuse for aggression to the Chinese (who had already made up their minds to go on the offensive long back, but also presented a fait accompli to the government. When the Chinese came and surrounded the Oho-la post on September 8, the government was presented with a Hobson's choice. Neither could Nehru afford to be seen, by his domestic audience to be backing off **in** the face of aggression, nor could he allow the

Chinese to think that India had feet of clay, when the chips were down.

Portrait of Lt Gen Kunwar Umrao Singh Nathawat (Image via indianrajputs.com)

What we have said above, of course, does not absolve higher echelons from their despicable indecision and leader-ship failure. Three months after the Thag-la opportunity was missed by local commands and the infringement of the McMahon Line (Dho-la post) happened with a casual air, Eastern Army Commander got into the act. On November 13,

1962, Sen, Eastern Army GOC-in-C, held a meeting at Tezpur with Nathawat, GOC XXXIII Corps, and Parshad, GOC 4 Division, among others.

With a straight face, he said that the Indian government had always considered the watershed principle as the basis for the correct alignment of the McMahon Line.

[Note: Sen had come to Tezpur via Delhi, where he at- tended a meeting on October 12, chaired by Menon, the de- fence minister. What are the odds that his sudden enthusiasm for the watershed

principle, was born out of some reassurance he had received from that exalted company in Delhi? It is immensely unfortunate and irregular as a procedure that Menon had insisted that no minutes would be kept of his meetings, purportedly of their sensitive nature. So, very conveniently for some, evidence of all moronic wrongdoings and blunders are buried forever in the maze of "I said-he said".]

(a) Physical contact with DHOLA must be made.

(b) Government would not accept any intrusion of the Chinese into our territory. If they come in, they must be thrown out by force. In this context, Chief of the Army Staff had ordered the Army Commander to stress that "No weakness will be shown". This was, therefore, reflected in Eastern Command signal of 9 September 1962.

(c) The Army Commander felt that there was some doubt in the minds of officers regarding the alignment of the McMAHON Line WEST of KHINZEMANE. He clarified that the Government had always maintained that McMAHON Line was based on the watershed principle and, therefore, it ran along the THAGLA Ridge. Thus DHOLA was well inside the McMAHON Line.

(d) The Army Commander then stated that he had pointed out at DELHI that we must expect reactions by the Chinese along NEFA/TIBET Border, where our garrisons were relatively weak compared to the Chinese. Government had accepted this, but, at the same time, directed that, should any of our posts be lost, every effort will be made to retake them. The DIB who was at the meeting in DELHI, in this connection had stated that he considered that the likely Chinese targets would be TAKSING, MECHUKA, and TUTING. The Chief of the Army Staff had then directed that, with the move of 62 Infantry Brigade to NEFA, these places would be reinforced as under:-

(i) TUTING to be made up to a battalion strength.

(ii) TAKSING to be reinforced by a company.

HBR

But true to our approach for this story, of sticking to documented evidence and first-person accounts only, it stands to reason that Sen had no clarity about any realignment of the

McMahon Line (vis-a-vis the original line on the map) prior to this date.

As records suggest, his earlier studied silence on all clarifications sought by local formations, bear testimony to this. What is particularly painful, is the leadership failure.

A genuine lack of certainty about the McMahon Line, under those chaotic circumstances, is understandable. What is galling is the attempt to palm off the blame to lower formations by saying "there are some doubts in the minds of officers regarding the alignment of the McMahon Line west of Khinzemane".

If Sen took responsibility for the earlier confusion in June, about the alignment of the McMahon Line, he would then also have had to take responsibility for the consequences of not occupying Thag-la in time. As a military man he would then not be able to disregard the tactical implications of hostile occupation of Thag-la so coolly when he thundered "they must be thrown out by force" (please see the image above from the Henderson Brooks report).

Thus, we can clearly see that India erred both politically and militarily in its defence of the McMahon Line in Nefa's Namka-chu area.

Many commentators and a large section of Indians believe that the military should be "unshackled" and allowed to play a larger, more decisive, role in geostrategic decision-making. That constituency would perhaps feel differently about the conclusions arrived at, in this fact-finding long read.

[Note: There are historical instances demonstrating the consequences of military-dictated, precipitate action in international relations, particularly in explosive situations [R13]

Having said that the Indian Army was at fault militarily in Nefa, let us take our readers to a closer examination of other possible options, the Army had in the Kameng Frontier Division, on the ground, that fateful summer and autumn of 1962. In geostrategic policymaking, there is a school of thought that endorses preemptive military action in "national interest", even if these are questionable legally and morally.

Israel has been a consistent practitioner of this doctrine. They have often broken international law and transgressed considerations of morality, to protect their "national interests".

Here we are not including mega events like the illegal US war against Iraq in 2004 or the Soviet Union's imperialistic aggression against Afghanistan in 1979. We are limiting ourselves to preemptive occupation of foreign territory, adjoining one's borders, for proactively protecting the nation's vital interests - something like Israel's operations inside Lebanon's southern borders, in order to protect northern Israeli territory from militant and rocket attacks.

In the long run, these Israeli operations came to a dead end and had to be wound down. But they had met limited goals in the short term, for some years. Could the Army try anything like that in Nefa in 1962 in "national interest"?

The agitated reaction to this query would be one of incredulity and indignation. There is no comparison between the balance of military power that Israel had with Hezbollah in Lebanon and what India had with China at any stage.

But then what went into the thinking when the XXXIII Corps, 4 Division and their officers took liberties across the McMahon Line, casually and tried to drive these legal factors under the carpet? And, if they took those liberties in the national interest, one would assume that they were trying to protect India's strategic, operational, and political interests in those circumstances of uncertainty?

As things turned out, India was prepared to deploy a brigade on and around the McMahon Line with artillery sup- port. Prasad's warning about the unsustainability of an FDL at Thag-la or Dho-la, presumed company level resources stretching across that entire theatre. However, since four battalions were available to be deployed in that immediate area, then both Karpo-la II and Namdang-la could have been covered to protect the flanks of any FDL on the Thag-la ridge?

In that case why didn't they occupy the Thag-la Ridge which tactically dominated the entire Namka-chu valley, be- tween the India-Bhutan-Tibet trijunction and the Namka- chu (river)- Niyamjang-chu (river) confluence? The Hathung- la ridge to the south of the confluence was, after all, firmly in Indian control and dominated the Niyamjang-chu valley to

the north. For decades, commentators have speculated that occupation of the Thag-la ridge would have given the Indian post command of both these valleys - and the Sumdorong- chu valley further east.

A bird's eye view of the entire sector, from the frontier areas up to Tawang, as seen from the Tibetan side

In the "what if" scenario, even though Prasad didn't occupy Thag-la based on his perspective in May-June 1962, what stopped 7 Brigade or 4 Division from ordering it, once Prasad returned and made his report?

The tactical riddle with a strategic flavour- neither cautious legality nor military boldness through pre-emptive intrusion?

The Thag-la heights remained free of the PLA for many weeks after Prasad's return. Niranjan Parshad's griping to Kaul in October, over Thag-la made no sense at all since by setting up the post at Tse-dong (Dho-la post), the McMahon Line on the map had anyway been transgressed. So, what was this squeamishness about going in a bit deeper, and climbing the next height (nine more miles on the ground)?

If the Army sat atop the Thag-la ridge and its adjoining passes, legally or not, would then the subsequent "outflanking, infiltration and envelopment" manoeuvre that the PLA used against 7 Brigade on October 20, have been possible?

We have seen that most military narratives on the Namka-chu debacle, have held that, as what made the fatal difference. To reiterate our proposition: Do remember, AHQ had permitted the setting up of posts on the McMahon Line without prior sanction, vide their April 27 Memo.

We haven't been able to find any credible or rational answers to this. The local commanders all blame the AHQ and the Eastern Army for not responding to their queries about the occupation of Thag-la, while there was time. However, none explain why the AHQ's concurrence became vital for Thag-la but not for transgressing the McMahon Line beyond Tsangdhar, and setting up the Dho-la post.

If they could do it at Dho-la (Tse Dong) why not at Thag-la?

As we concluded earlier, we can now reiterate it and say that the Army's command failure was without any rational reason on both political and military considerations. Then, was it really Thag-la that made the difference on 20 October 1962?

Enough time and words have been spent on the tactical disadvantages of the Dho-la post, the vulnerability of the Namka-chu "shooting gallery" and the Thag-la lament. However, on the day of action, how decisive were these fac- tors? On that morning of October 20, 1962, were *these* factors responsible for the decimation of unit after unit in the Namka-chu valley, in the Dho-la post, and up on the Tsangdhar ridge? Or is it part of the larger myth-making that surrounds the Namka-chu debacle?

20TH OCTOBER 1962, THE DAY OF RECKONING; THE CHINESE PLAN AND EXECUTION; WHO DID WHAT ON THE INDIAN SIDE; THE TALES OF GLORY AND DISGRACE; AT WHOSE DOOR DOES THE SHAME LIE?

Let us step back a minute, from this exclusive focus on the Indian side of the story. Let us see what 7 Brigade was up against, on the Chinese side.

What were the PLA's plans, their strength on the ground, what tactics they followed and how the viewed the Indian combat performance? This may show us a mirror on our brigade- and unit-level tactical performance.

Was the Indian army tactically sound and effective? Was the bravery and sacrifice of the Indian troops backed up by sound defensive plans, leadership, and tactics from their commanders?

The Chinese version of the battle-plans and execution in actual combat; acknowledgement of 2 Rajput's in- credible heroism

We are quoting below a not-so-good translation of an interview of Lieutenant General Yin Fa Tang, who in 1962 served as the political commissar of PLA's "Tibetan Army, Formation 419".

Interview published in the second issue of the "Military History" magazine of the Academy of Military Sciences, China, in 2005.

The interviewer is Colonel Wei Bihai, deputy director, PLA's

History Research Office. We have spared readers the Chinese political narrative that inevitably colours such pieces in a totalitarian country and just presented the military, operational, and tactical aspects of the interview:

PLA Lt Gen Yin Fa Tang (Photo credit: Unknown Chinese photographerlwww.tibetology.ac.cn)

Wei Bihai: *You are "Old Tibet". From the Battle of Qamdo in 1950 to 1985, six years after reform and opening up, Tibet experi- enced tremendous changes and many major historical events with far-reaching influence. You have all experienced them. As a history researcher, I have too many questions to ask you. In view of the time limit, this time I will talk about one question-the formation of Tibetan 419 Troops.*

Yin Fa Tang: *The "Tibetan 419 Unit" was not originally a unit but the code name of a command headquarters called the:Advance Command of the Tibet Military Region". This headquarters was formed in June 1962. At that time, the*

Tibet Military Region had only three regiments in the field. 419 commanded these three regiments to prepare for the armed conflict on the Sino-Indian border.

Later, the command headquarters and its troops took part in the Sino-Indian border self-defence counterattack as troops equivalent to a division. By June 1963, the code name "Tibetan Unit 419" was cancelled, and it had existed for about a year. It can be said that the "Tibetan Unit 419" was formed temporarily to cope with the escalating armed conflict on the Sino-Indian border.

Wei: *I heard that before the Battle of Kejielang (Chinese name for the Namka-chu area), the commander of Unit 419, especially you, gave very good suggestions on the decision-making of the bat- tle. Please talk about the situation in this regard.*

Yin: *The frontline commanders should not mechanically execute orders from their superiors. They should follow the spirit of the Gutian Conference, put forward their own opinions based on the actual situation, and have the courage to make comments. This is also the old tradition of our People's Liberation Army, especially the 18th Army. As mentioned earlier, Commander Zhang Guohua's sug- gestions for changes to the general staff's combat plan is a shining example.*

At that time, the Indian 7th Brigade's deployment in the Khjielang (Namka-chu) area was like a short-legged "T". The front was wide, with shallow depth, and each stronghold was close to each other. If one of their battalions was annihilated, it is possible for the others to escape. Since we had the ability to destroy them, it is better to make a plan to wipe out the entire brigade. Fighting a brigade is a fight and fighting a battalion is also a fight. Fighting piecemeal actions against their battalions is more troublesome. It is better to fight a brigade with full intensity.

In fact, in this battle, commanders at all levels had put forward very good suggestions. For example, the military area pointed out that the original task given to the 155th Regiment of the main at- tacking force was to first annihilate the enemies of the Kalong stronghold (between Bridge IV and Bridge VI}, and then to wipe out the enemies gun positions (artillery and heavy mortars on the Tsangdhar ridge) and other strongholds. In the 155th Regiment area, since Kalong is very close to the gun positions, the assault group must be accompanied by forces outflanking the enemy's line (across the log bridge and area to its west) to attack their gun positions (on Tsangdhar ridge). They believed that they were capable of destroying these two strongholds at the same time, so they took the initiative to advise their superiors.

Chai Hongquan and Shi Banqiao (previously referred to as the deputy chief of staff of the military region) went to the 155th Regiment for inspection. The head of regiment Liu Guangtong and political commissar Qiao Xueting made this proposal to them. Chai and Shi did not agree. Later, I went to the 155 Unit and they suggested to me that my thinking makes sense and can be adopted. I asked Chai Hongquan that Chai didn't make a statement. He asked Shi Banqiao, Shi was not easy to say. I will report directly to Commander Zhang Guohua. Commander Zhang took it very seriously and called me directly to ask me, is it sure that the two strongholds will fight together? I have a better understanding of the situation of this unit, so I replied that there is no problem and I am sure. Commander Zhang decisively made the decision and approved the proposal of the 155 regiment. There are such cases.

Our participating forces were all the 419 Unit troops, the 2nd Battalion of the 32nd Regiment of the 11th Division, the 1st Shannan Army Division and one artillery and one engineering unit, which was a total of 10,300 (soldiers). Our strength ratio with the enemy was 3:1 - we are three times the enemy. Commander Zhang Guohua authorized the 419 Unit command organization to command the abovementioned participating units. The front finger of the Tibet Military Region was in Ma Ma, and the 419 Command office was in Xuebo Cave.

Wei: *Please talk about the history of the Battle of Kejielang (Namka-chu).*

Yin: The Battle of Kejielang (Namka-chu) was the first battle in the Sino-Indian border self-defence counterattack, and it was also the fiercest and most difficult battle. Before the war, commanders at all *levels carried out repeated reconnaissance of the enemy's situation and terrain, studied and formulated very detailed combat plans based on actual conditions. After the Indian Army launched continuous attacks on us, we launched a self-defence counterattack in the early morning of October 20th. Our army adopts the tactics of night and dawn attacks, infiltrated under the cover of night, penetrated the enemy's flanks and rear areas, and waited in hiding at the start- ing points of the attack.*

The task of attacking the right wing of the Indian Army (Khinzemane post and the Niyamjang-chu valley route) was basically performed by the 154 Regiment alone. The 155 Regiment at- tacked the left-wing Karon (Bridge IV to the temporary log bridge) and the gun positions of the Indian Army (on the Tsangdhar ridge) with the cooperation of the 157 regiment (they went across west of the log bridge) ... a battalion of the 32nd Regiment of the 11th Division and the Shannan Army Division, launched an attack on the two positions of the Indian Army at 7.30 (?) in the morning.

*The Chinese regiments segmented the battl,efield. Indian l,eft flank was **infiltrated** at night and the positions of 2 Rajput attacked from all sides in the morning. Then the Chinese moved up the Tsangdhar slopes and overwhelmed the paltry defences there. The right flank was penetrated along the Niyamjung chu valley but 6 Indian companies (of 9 Punjab and 4 Grenadiers) around bridges I & II not significantly engaged on 20th.*

CHINESE ATTACK 20 OCTOBER

14. The 1000 - 1200 Chinese force moving towards TSANGIE on 19 October and the force that collected in SINGJANG during night 19/20 October crossed the River line between the log Bridge and Bridge 5 before dawn of 20 October. The total strength of the combined force was perhaps a regiment. A battalion of this force went straight for TSANGDHAR.

15. The remainder formed up just before dawn WEST of the RAJPUT Position in the FUP Nullah. The H Hour for the attack was first light, which was approximately 0500 hours. For twenty minutes before H Hour, there was heavy shelling on the RAJPUT and GORKHA positions; the preliminary softening up before the attack. At H Hour, under cover of an artillery barrage, the Chinese attacked the RAJPUTS from the WEST flank and, after severe hand-tohand fighting, rolled up the RAJPUT position by 0715 hours.

16. Part of this force moved parallel but SOUTH of the RAJPUT Position and gave flank protection to the attacking force. This flank protection force met the ASSAM Rifles post SOUTH of Bridge 4 at about 0430 hours and overran them. On RAJPUT Position falling, the Chinese battalions facing the RAJPUTS from NORTH of the River crossed over and, by 0830 hours, captured 1/9 GORKHA RIFLES Positions and Bridge 3.

17. All the while our remaining positions from Bridge 3 to Bridge 1 were being engaged by the Chinese positions facing them on the NORTH of the NAMKA CHU.

18. With 2 RAJPUT and 1/9 GORKHA RIFLES gone, the Brigade Headquarters was in danger of being overrun. The Brigade Commander, therefore, decided to fall back in line with TSANGDHAR. But, in the meantime, the Chinese battalion, detached before dawn for TSANGDHAR, had moved up and, by 1000 hours, TSANGDHAR Dropping Zone was in Chinese hands. We had few defences in TSANGDHAR and the only troops there were those on Dropping Zone duties.

HBR
To be honest, the Indian Army was still very capable of fighting. They were the elite of the Indian Army, and they were deceived by propaganda, thinking that our army had invaded Indian territory, and they didn't understand our army's particularly brave fighting style and POW (prisoner of war) policy, so they just resisted blindly and defended the bunkers.

They suffered more deaths than the number of prisoners taken by us. For example, there were 143 Indian soldiers in the Kalong stronghold, of which 92 were killed by our army, and only 51 were taken prisoners, many of whom were captured because of injuries. Our army suffered more casualties in the battle to conquer Caron, sacrificed 21 people and wounded 29 people.

Wei: *When the two strong meet, the brave wins [Sic]_ It should be said that the tenacity of our army overwhelmed the Indian army.*

Yin: *That's pretty good. The fortifications of the Indian Army were* *mainly bunkers. For example, in the Karon stronghold, with 143 Indian soldiers, 64 bunkers were built. Our army was attacking point by point from bunker to bunker. That's really short-handed. The famous "Yangtingan Class" emerged during this battle. The squad had a total of eight people. The squad leader died, and the second squad leader went on to command; the second squad leader died, and the deputy squad leader immediately went up; the deputy squad leader died, and the veterans immediately went up, and fi- nally sacrificed 7 people, leaving only one recruit. This recruit took the initiative to join another squad to continue fighting, really going forward. With the cooperation of another squad, this squad con- quered 27 bunkers and wiped out 55 enemies. After the war, it was awarded the honorary title by the (Chinese) national defence ministry.*

Where has the Indian Army seen such a powerful unit? We re- ally overwhelmed them in momentum. Our army completed the three-day tough task, which was originally scheduled, in just one day. Most of the 7th Brigade of the Indian Army was annihilated at that time, and the rest was scattered in the jungle. Soon after, we cleared it out, and finally the entire brigade was annihilated. In the following battles, the morale of the Indian Army was completely dis- integrated, and their army was really devastated.

***

Somewhere in the din of macrolevel issues of maps, memos, policies, and politics we lose sight of what actually happened on the ground, on the day of reckoning. The above

Chinese account matches the version laid out by several military analysts and researchers from the Indian side. But the distinct advantage of reading the Chinese account is to see the battle without the background filters.

When you read Indian accounts, by the time you arrive at the actual battle on October 20, 1962, you are already heavily weighed down by factors like the domination of the PLA positions on the Thag-la ridge and the shortage of ammunition and supplies. But in the actual event, which factor(s) turned out to be decisive?

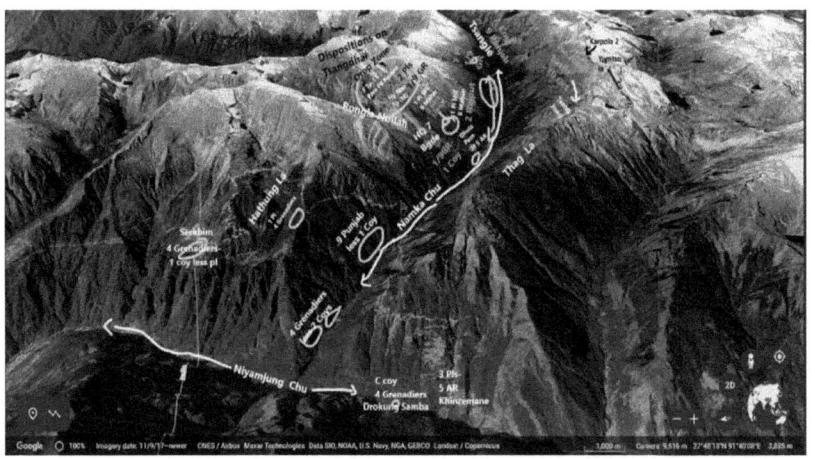

Indian positions in the two river valleys and on the overlooking ridges, morning of 20 October, the day of the Chinese attack. 10th October battle location marked for perspective. The positions have been marked from details given in the official history. However, HBR gives a slightly different deployment, putting 1/9 GR, less company and a platoon (instead of just that 1 coy as shown here), as brigade reserve in the Rongla area. The latter seems less probable when referenced with other events and accounts.

From a classical military doctrinal perspective, it is a no-brainer that if the enemy occupies higher terrain facing your positions and you are short of supplies, you will lose, unless help arrives. But is that what happened on the morning of the October 20? What difference would it have made if the Indian troops had ammunition and enough food? How did the Thag-la advantage eventually play out in the Chinese plan of attack and its execution?

For our readers let us simplify what happened.

The Chinese 155 Regiment plus some troops from the 157 infiltrated at night, between the Indian positions on the left. They reached vantage points *behind* 2 Rajput's positions and waited for "H-Hour" - the time of day at which an attack, landing, or other military operation is scheduled to begin.

After a brief bombardment in the morning, their troops were in and among our positions willy-nilly. The fighting was at close quarters and very soon it was a vicious hand-to-hand fight to the finish.

Other troops from the 157 Regiment had come across the low flowing river on the left and moved up slopes of the Tsangdhar heights, overwhelmed the 1/9 GR companies and stormed the Indian artillery and mortar positions, along with our air-resupply zones.

The Chinese account explicitly mentions, somewhat in awe, the dogged and suicidal nature of the Indian resistance, in these hopeless last-ditch actions!

In the meantime, the Chinese 154 Regiment rolled up our positions on the right, from the direction of the Niyamjang- chu valley. Similar outflanking manoeuvre, putting their troops behind our positions.

[Note: The lack of reserves behind the Indian FDL for local interception and counterattacks at the unit level as well as at the brigade level.]

Who lost the battle on the Indian side - at whose door does the shame lie? Demolishing the myths and folk-lore; the officers who let down their men, army and nation.

We have been advised by "thinking" and conscientious, senior commanders, that under the specific circumstances that Parshad and Dalvi found themselves in, they could have interpreted their orders liberally and redeployed their forces in a viable defensive mode, while covering the river and its crossings. Operation Leghorn (the offensive on Thag la) had been called off and the units (except 1/9 GR less coy) were strung out along the Namka chu valley, line abreast. After all, no order did, or could, require a brigade, facing an enemy force, to NOT deploy tactically in defence!

The HBR does mention that "the Corps Commander insisted there will be no 'thinning out' from DHOLA area" (ref: HBR para no., 74 quoted previously). A viable defensive line requires reserves in depth, mutually supporting defended locations and effective patrolling of gaps in between locations. Here, except those 3 Companies of 1/9 GR (one coy having been deployed to cover the Brigade HQ at Rongla nullah), no infantry was held back on the Tsangdhar slopes or heights. Thus, there was neither any defence in depth nor any viable, mobile force for interdicting or counter attacking the enemy's lines of advance. And, as already noted previously, there was no night patrolling of the vital 10 km gap between the last temporary (log) bridge and bridge V at the extreme left flank.

Commanders in battle, down the ages, have discovered that "no plan of operations survives, with any certainty, be- yond the first encounter with the enemy's main force [F8]." Some commanders get overwhelmed by this dissonance while others use it to their advantage. After all the enemy too is subject to this dictum. So, the "no thinning out" instruction need not, on the ground, compel a commander to dump fundamental infantry tactics.

When Chinese troop movements towards forward stag- ing areas (see **HBR** image below) were clearly visible on October 19, their intentions towards an imminent offensive should have been clear.

> 12. Apart from the dumping and the build up seen on the THAGLA Ridge, there were other activities that indicated that the Chinese might force a show down in the near future, if NOT the next day. Some 1000 to 1200 Chinese were seen moving across towards SINGJANG - TSANGLE Area. The Brigade Commander appreciated that either this force would attack TSANGLE or drive a wedge through the Brigade defences to TSANGDHAR. He, therefore, warned all commanding officers to be vigilant and, in particular, the TSANGLE troops.

Dalvi claims to have known that his line abreast dispositions would be penetrated and overwhelmed easily. Strangely, even after surmising that the PLA may be aiming for penetrating his left flank to have a go for his artillery and supply base on Tsangdhar, he didn't detail any troops to watch over the likely ingress routes across the, by now ford- able river, and its south bank. There was a 10 km gap be- tween the temporary bridge (on his left flank) and bridge V!

This collective obsession with Tsangle, at this late stage, is amazing!

The PLA were swarming all over the Thag-la ridge line and the passes on it. The Army had given up all hopes of an offensive up to that ridge line. So, what was now the tactical criticality of Tsangle? In the actual event, the PLA though keeping up a steady barrage on 9 Punjab's positions there, never physically stormed the Punjabi company!

So, we can see, Dalvi and his boss, Parshad watched all this happening. Griped and argued for 10 days but actually did nothing. Even after all offensive intentions had been given up by higher command, the local commanders, did not make any attempts to organise defensive positions in their AOR (are of responsibility). They saw the Chinese build up and offensive preparations and then they argued and complained some more!

What were they waiting for? Where was their professional military man's conscience and sense of accountability to their men and task a hand? There are plenty of instances in military history, where local commanders or juniors in positions where they could make a difference, have liberally interpreted their orders, when compelling circumstances so demanded, on the ground [F4].

Seeing Parshad's later conduct under fire, in the next war (September 6-7, 1965, as GOC of 15 Division on Wagah-Lahore axis), it can be safely said that the man didn't have what it takes to command troops in action [F5].

The job of a commander is to meet the objective of an operation and look after his men and equipment in the process. Can a commander plead helplessness later while interpreting his orders literally and knowingly courting disaster? Whether that would have materially changed the out- come is another matter, but a better fight may have been given. Defeat need not have been so quick, comprehensive and humiliating.

The impact of Dalvi and Parshad's indecisiveness and command failures, on the morale and motivation of their officers and men, lie embedded in how the battle unfolded. Apart from the brave, last ditch stand of 2 Rajput in the morning, the other units simply disintegrated or were swept aside, barring isolated instances of grit and courage.

Brigadier Dalvi being taken Prisoner Of War, on 21 October (Photo credit: Unknown Chinese photographer/ zhuanlan.zhihu.com)

In this context, let us look at the curious developments on the right flank of Dalvi's defences, east of Rongla Nullah and Bridge-III, after his command collapsed in the morning and he fled into the heights. Both, 9 Punjab (less coy) and 4 Grenadiers (less 2 coys), at bridges II and I respectively, had been only partially engaged in the morning of 20th, except for B coy, 4 Grenadiers, near Bridge- I, which took casualties. Maj General Parshad, who had direct communications intact with these units, ordered them to give up their positions by the river and climb up to Hathung la (right behind them). 9 Punjab received the order at llOO hrs and had successfully disengaged by 1430. While the Grenadiers were asked to hold on till 1700 and then fall back.

> The CO of 9 Punjab apprised the GOC 4 Inf Div of the situation at the Namkha Chu at 1030 hrs, after which the GOC ordered CO 9 Punjab at about 1100 hrs to withdraw the Bn and take up a lay back position at Hathongla. Withdrawal was to take place along the ridge and not along the track to avoid enemy interference. The Battalion started withdrawal at 1200 hrs and completed it by 1430 hrs. By this time the Chinese had started shelling Bridge 2 positions and also formed up on the north bank of the river for assault(153).

Official history

Yet we find that they had not reached Hathung-la even next morning (though there were pathways leading up to the ridge line behind them) and the lone platoon atop the ridge was quickly overrun by the Chinese.

> The next day the enemy started attacking Hathongla at 0500 hrs and shelling Chuthangmu at 0530 hrs while Brokenthang was brought under fire at about 0625 hrs. One platoon of 4 Grenadiers, which was positioned at Hathongla on 20 October, was in no position to offer any resistance to the enemy and it was over-powered in their first assault. Considering

Official history

It is to be noted that the Chinese did not press any attack since evening of 20th till 0500 hours on 21st. So there possibly couldn't be any interference with the two Indian units' attempts to reach Hathung-la ridge behind their positions. Yet this is what we find about 9 Punjab and 4 Grenadiers around evening on 21st!

Official history

> D Coy of 4 Grenadiers, less platoon, which was located at Serkhim, held on to their position till 0930 hrs. But when they received reports of enemy advancing towards their position and seeing Lumpo in flames, the troops vacated their position of their own (159). The main battalion (consisting of Commanding Officer, A and B Coys and part of Adm Coy which was positioned at Bridge 1 was still in the area, searching for a safe track downward, when they were met somewhere near Hathongla by Lt Col R.N. Mishra, CO 9 Punjab, with a handful of his Jawans, at 2000 hrs on 21 October.

There were others who simply remained absent in action! For instance, the curious experience of the men of the 1/9 GR

> The 1/9 GR platoon, which was positioned on the track Tsangdhar-Bridge 5, was subjected to heavy shelling. The OC 'A' Coy, Maj A.G. Minwalla, who was heading this platoon, went ahead with a few of his men to Bridge 5 but found the position abandoned by the Coy of 9 Punjab. Seeing the Chinese coming in mass, Maj Minwalla returned. He did not return to Nelum, where he had left the other soldiers of his platoon, but crossed into Bhutan. The men at Nelum were left to care for themselves. Some of them returned to Lumpo while others crossed into Bhutan.

platoon posted at Nelum (on the track from Tsangdhar to bridge V) under Major A.G. Minwalla, OC, A coy. This officer asked the men to hang on, under shelling and went ahead to bridge V to ascertain what was going on. Upon finding the bridge area abandoned by A coy, 9 Punjab, he too made off to Bhutan, without informing the platoon he had left behind, simply abandoning his men!

Official history

For the sake of perspective, we must also note that for all the talk, on the Indian side, about terrain, logistics and difficult going in this sector, the Chinese seemed to be impervious to all these "difficulties"! With full battle loads, supplies and supporting arms, they crossed the Tsangdhar and Karpola-I 'humps' in half a day, between the afternoon of 20th and first light of 21st. And then they reached Tawang town in three days, early on the 24th of October. Just like they were able to construct a military road from Bumla to Tawang in three weeks, after the October battles, before resuming their operations in November! Something which eluded the Indians for three months before the October battles!

In this context, readers should also note that while 7 Brigade collapsed like a bag of wind at Namka chu, in the same period, under the command of Brigadier Kalyan Singh, 4 Artillery Brigade, responsible for the Tawang area, 1 Sikh with the help of 7 Mountain (Bengal) Battery, gave a far better account of themselves. Deployed on the Bum la - 1B Ridge - Tongpeng la- Milaktong la axis, north of Tawang,. This unit held the Chinese back at Tongpeng la till ordered to fall back, protesting all the way at having to give up a victorious defensive battle, retreated in good order to Tawang, with all equip- ment, modest casualties and still full of fight! The collapse of 7 Brigade on the left flank severely impacted Brigadier Kalyan Singh's positions.

This goes to show that there was nothing inherently wrong with our troops deployed in the Tawang sector. Leadership, planning and tactical deployment made a significant difference.

As a sad footnote to this story, we must add that while the careers and reputations of the top brass like Kaul may have had to "lie down on the beds they, themselves, made", they did live on to write their memoirs and ruminate on whatcould have been. As did Niranjan Parshad and Brigadier Dalvi. They got away with their excuses and sad alibis of "interference" from and ineptitude of their seniors.

But one officer literally did lie down on the bed of his own making. The fall guy - Captain Mahavir Prasad had been deputed to 1/9 GR from his original unit. Lt General Kaul had asked Major General Parshad to lend his nephew, Captain Prasad to 7 Brigade, from 1 Sikh which was deployed on the

Tawang - Bum la axis, under the command of Brigadier Kalyan Singh's 4 Artillery Brigade. Kaul wanted an officer with thorough knowledge of the Namka chu sector, to be at hand. He was given the field rank of Major and sent back to the same locale, where, as the first representative of the Indian army ever to set foot, he had visited earlier that year, in May - June.

Thus, by a cruel stroke of fate, he ended up defending a position on October 20, which, in his original assessment, was "suicidal". Just as he had predicted in June that year, the Dhola post and our defences around it were infiltrated and penetrated in no time. He reportedly fell in an enemy as- sault, manning a Bren gun whose original gunner had al- ready been killed [R14]

The Calcutta boy, Prasad, didn't live to tell his tale or re- veal the complete reality of Namka-chu, which was cremated along with his body. He fell fighting that morning, among the dense foliage and on the soggy ground, he had patrolled so extensively just four months ago. As was the fate of so many of his brother officers and men, of 2 Rajput for instance, who, according to the Chinese account above, fell where they stood, rather than surrender.

The senior officers lived on to tell their tales, the incomplete stories absolving themselves of all responsibility for the disaster. Like Prasad's uncle, Major General Niranjan Parshad, [F6] GOC, 4 division, and his brigade commander John Dalvi and the oh-so-innocent GOC, IV corps, Lieutenant General Kaul.

And side by side with the acts of heroism we may have certain 'myths of heroism' too. Awards given, hagiographies created, without reference to actual facts and deeds.

It is important that the complete truth about these wars, in which people die, are known and analysed. More than celebrating the victories, it is critical to understand the reversals and then act on such understanding. Otherwise, we will have a never-ending caravan of Namka-chu (1962) and

IPKF (1987-1990) and Kargil (1999) and Galwan (2020) and the perpetual blood letting inKashmir's counterinsurgency operations.

"The entire deaths of Vietnam died in vain. And they're dying in vain right this very second. And you know what's worse than a soldier dying in vain? It's more soldiers dying in vain. That's what's worse." -
Mike Gravel

Mentions:

{M1} "The Himalayan Blunder" by Brigadier John Dalvi.

*{M2} "The Battle of Tawang" by Major General **KK** Tewari.*

{M3} "1962 War: Battle of Namka Chu - As I Saw It" by Brigadier A.J.S. Behl.

References & Bibliography:

{R1} From Wu Lengxi's book- "Shi nian lunzhan, 1956-1966, Zhong Su guanxi huiyilu" (Ten-Year War of Words, 1956-1966, a Memoir of Sino-Soviet Relations)

that said: "After the Tibetan insurgency against the Chinese began in Lhasa on 10 March 1959, on 25 March, the CCP's (Communist Party of China's) top leaders discussed this issue with all its implications. According to Chairman Mao, India was at fault and was instigating the Tibetan rebellion. He directed that India wouldn't be confronted at that moment but would be taught a lesson later, after India further aggravated the situation through her own doings."

{R2} "New Directions in the Study of China's Foreign Policy - China's Decision for War with India in 1962" by John W Garver.

{R3} "Indian spymaster Mullik (BN) quietly reaffirmed his tacit approval of the agency's (CIA's) efforts in 1961 and had earlier claimed that Nehru held similar beliefs."-From "The CJA's Secret War in Tibet" by Kenneth Conboy and James Morrison.

{R4}"The Untold Story" by Lt Gen Brij Mohan Kaul has been referred to for his version of events as explained in the relevant sections of this story.

{R5}"The Henderson Brooks Report" that was "leaked" by Neville

Maxwell. [Note1: We have deliberately left out Neville Maxwell's analysis and perspective from India's China war, unless the same is corroborated by other sources. His role and doings in India as the South Asian correspondent of The

*Times were curious to say the least. He had disgraced himself as an analyst and scholar of any consequence, when he predicted that the 1967 parliamentary election would be India's last democratic election and the country's democracy would collapse after that. Moreover, while he made full use of the relatively free ambience in India, to the extent of acquiring a copy of the, then classified and unobtainable, Henderson Brooks Report on the India-China war, he had absolutely no independent insight into the Chinese side of things, apart from official communiques and biased private briefings. Therefore, we consider his work as an incomplete treatise, prejudiced and blind to one set of facts - the facts from China's side. However, we have used Maxwell's "leaked" copy of the Henderson Brooks Report for much of our referencing on the Indian Army's decisions, orders, reports, and opinions, apart from other sources for first-hand reports, from participants like Lt Gen BM Kaul's - "The Untold Story" and Brig John Dalvi's "The Himalayan Blunder". We consider his copy of the **HBR** authentic since the Indian government immediately banned his book - "India's China War" - in 1970 because it quoted the **HBR** and declared him a proclaimed offender under the Official Secrets Act. This indirectly confirms that his copy of the **HBR** was genuine.]*

*[Note:2 The Morarji Desai government withdrew the charges in 1978. Hence, the criminalization of the event has long been rendered null and void. With the recent publication of the **HBR** in Maxwell's website and numerous copies circulated on the internet, the matter of the OSA (Official Secrets Act) violation is now dead.]*

{R6} The Official Indian History of the 1962 war with China - "History of the Conflict with China, 1962" by Dr. PB Sinha and Colonel AA Athale.

{R7} 1962- *The Battle of Namka Chu and Fall of Tawang (A View from the Other Side of the Hill)*, Major General P.J.S. Sandhu (retired.)

{R8} SJB.N. Mullik, then Director- Intelligence Bureau of India, in: *"My Years with Nehru - The Chinese Betrayal"*.

{R9} Since the India-China border dispute is historically linked to "differing perceptions", it is important to note that in Neja, the McMahon Line is a clearly drawn boundary, whose wisdom and methodology may be disputed on technical grounds, but not its location on the map. The Shim/a Convention of 1914, between British India, Tibetan government, and its sovereign overlord- Republic of China, produced this boundary with clearly laid down coordinates. Subsequently the pre- communist Chinese government disputed that part of the agreement which dealt with the demarcation of the areas under the Tibetan government's authority (the blue line) and those directly under Chinese administration. /This was the reason why Ivan Chen, the Chinese representative, didn't sign the final agreement.] However, the part demarcating the India-Tibet border (the red line, which is also known as the McMahon Line) over 890 kilometres from the north-eastern extremity of Bhutan to the Isu-Razi pass on the Burma (now Myanmar) border, remained undisputed between the respective signatories - Henry McMahon, foreign secretary of British India and Lonchen Satra, representative from the Tibetan government.

{R10} From sources who, on condition of anonymity, threw light on Captain Mahavir Prasad's observations and views on the Namka-chu area and the Dho-la post.

{R11} After the September 8 incident at the Dhola post, when Chinese forces surrounded the Assam Rifles platoon and India sent the 9 Punjab battalion in response, the conflict spiraled quickly. On September 22, the Chinese Communist Party's daily newspaper- People's Daily, printed an editorial titled "shi ke ren, shu bu ke ren" (if this can be tolerated, then what cannot be tolerated?). This paper was said to be under the direct supervision of historian and Maoist intellectual **Hu** Qiaomu. Hence, it's editorial content reflected the party's and government's thoughts at the highest level. John w Garver (ref., **Rl**) gives his take on the casus belli for the 1962 war, giving the details of why, how, by whom and when the Chinese decision was made.

{Rl2} Brigadier Indrajeet Gakhal (retired), of 1 Sikh kindly appeared in my video series, Sandy Wars, carried on the YouTube channel of India Sentinels, gave his analysis of Captain Mahavir Prasad's patrol.

{Rl3} The Schliejfen Plan during World War I and the French coup d'etats (in Algeria) of 1958 and 1961.

{Rl4} Major General Krishen Khorana (retired), from Captain Mahavir Prasad's unit, 1 Sikh, who fought in that battle, in October 1962 on the Bum la -Tawang axis, was Prasad's friend and colleague. He kindly appeared in my video series, Sandy Wars, carried on the YouTube channel of India Sentinels. He shared with me the ultimate heroic - tragic fate of (then) Major Prasad.

Footnotes:

[Fl] The "Chief of Army staff or COAS" has been referred to as "Army chief" in subsequent mentions.

[F2] During the subsequent engagements at the Sela front, in November, when Lt Gen Kaul resumed duties after his sick leave, Sikh troops started referring to him as the "marwan wala jarnal". Which is the Punjabi equivalent of the general who gets his people killed"! This reportedly impacted morale of the men.

[F3] "Thinning out" is a subjective term when applied to

frontline conditions. "*No plan of operations survives, with any certainty, beyond the first encounter with the enemy's main force*" was Prussian war guru, Field Marshal Helmuth von Moltke's sagely assertion in 1880 (Helmuth Graf von Moltke, *Militarische Werke, Kriegsgechichtliche Einzelschriften*).

[F4] A historical reference can be drawn from an incident during British General Claude Auchinlek Operation Crusader in North Africa, in 1941, when German General Erwin Rommel's operations officer, Siegfried Westphal, on his own risk, against Rommel's orders, recalled the 21 Panzer Division all the way back to the Tobruk front restoring a disastrous situation somewhat.

[F5] Western Army GOC-i11-C Lieutenant General Harbaksh Singh, in his book - "In the line of duty" - described Parshad's removal from command during a battle, in the early days of the India-Pakistan war of 1965, as: "We were directed by the divisional Military Police to the general officer commanding, Major General Niranjan Prashad, who was hiding in a recently irrigated sugarcane field. He came out to receive us, with his boots covered with wet mud. He had no headcover, nor was he wearing any badges of rank. He had stubble on his face, not having shaved, contrary to the custom before the start of an operation. Seeing him in such a state, the first question I asked him was whether he was the general officer commanding a (military) division or a coolie?"

[F6] Captain Mahavir Prasad was the nephew of Major General Niranjan Parshad. While Captain Prasad has been referred to as "Prasad" in this article, it should not be confused with "Parshad", which is used to refer to his uncle, Major General Niranjan Parshad.

About the author

Growing up in Rourkela, with a visible German population in the early years of the Steel Plant, the author developed an interest in World War II, its history and more. Many decades of study, in this fascinating domain, starting with 'war stories' and then pursuing it as a serious field of research, gave him significant expertise and specialization in this subject.

He wrote extensively on an international history forum dedicated to 'Axis History', for years. He tweets regularly on military history and analysis from the handle- libertariam96. It was on twitter that senior, retired officers of the Indian armed forces encouraged and advised him to take an interest in Indian Military History too. This led to his association with the defence &. strategic affairs website- India Sentinels, under his own name.

In recent years the author published highly appreciated articles, based on interviews with military participants and experts, on a range of stories like the Indian airborne operations in Maldives

(1988), a gallant sapper action in the Bangladesh war (1971), the exploits of the Indian Navy's Vikrant Battle Group, in forcing a favourable outcome in the east (1971), gripping accounts of battles on the LOC, in the Batalik (Kargil) area, under unfavourable conditions, amongst others.

Apart from military history, he actively engages in study, analysis and commentary on contemporary military matters, with particular focus on the 2020 Chinese incursions in Eastern Ladakh. He has done a number of interview-based articles and videos on this subject, on the India Sentinels website and their YouTube channel. The videos are to be found in the 'Sandy Wars' series of this channel.

The author is a management consultant by profession.

Ingram Content Group UK Ltd.
Milton Keynes UK
UKHW020707120723
424996UK00015B/410